Generalizability Theory: Inferences and Practical Applications

Leslie J. Fyans, Jr., *Editor*

NEW DIRECTIONS FOR TESTING AND MEASUREMENT

MICHAEL KEAN, *Editor-in-Chief*

Number 18, June 1983

Paperback sourcebooks in
The Jossey-Bass Social and Behavioral Sciences Series

Jossey-Bass Inc., Publishers
San Francisco • Washington • London

Leslie J. Fyans, Jr. (Ed.)
Generalizability Theory: Inferences and Practical Applications.
New Directions for Testing and Measurement, no. 18.
San Francisco: Jossey-Bass, 1983.

New Directions for Testing and Measurement Series
Michael Kean, *Editor-in-Chief*

New Directions for Testing and Measurement is published
quarterly by Jossey-Bass Inc., Publishers. Subscriptions, single-issue
orders, change of address notices, undelivered copies, and other
correspondence should be sent to *New Directions* Subscriptions,
Jossey-Bass Inc., Publishers, 433 California Street, San Francisco,
California 94104.

Editorial correspondence should be sent to the Editor-in-Chief,
Michael Kean, ETS, Evanston, Illinois 60201.

Library of Congress Catalogue Card Number LC 82-84214

International Standard Serial Number ISSN 0271-0633

International Standard Book Number ISBN 87589-902-1

Cover art by Willi Baum

Manufactured in the United States of America

Ordering Information

The paperback sourcebooks listed below are published quarterly and can be ordered either by subscription or single-copy.

Subscriptions cost $35.00 per year for institutions, agencies, and libraries. Individuals can subscribe at the special rate of $21.00 per year *if payment is by personal check.* (Note that the full rate of $35.00 applies if payment is by institutional check, even if the subscription is designated for an individual.) Standing orders are accepted. Subscriptions normally begin with the first of the four sourcebooks in the current publication year of the series. When ordering, please indicate if you prefer your subscription to begin with the first issue of the *coming* year.

Single copies are available at $7.95 when payment accompanies order, and *all single-copy orders under $25.00 must include payment.* (California, New Jersey, New York, and Washington, D.C., residents please include appropriate sales tax.) For billed orders, cost per copy is $7.95 plus postage and handling. (Prices subject to change without notice.)

Bulk orders (ten or more copies) of any individual sourcebook are available at the following discounted prices: 10–49 copies, $7.15 each; 50–100 copies, $6.35 each; over 100 copies, *inquire.* Sales tax and postage and handling charges apply as for single copy orders.

To ensure correct and prompt delivery, all orders must give either the *name of an individual* or an *official purchase order number.* Please submit your order as follows:

Subscriptions: specify series and year subscription is to begin.
Single Copies: specify sourcebook code (such as, TM8) and first two words of title.

Mail orders for United States and Possessions, Latin America, Canada, Japan, Australia, and New Zealand to:
Jossey-Bass Inc., Publishers
433 California Street
San Francisco, California 94104

Mail orders for all other parts of the world to:
Jossey-Bass Limited
28 Banner Street
London EC1Y 8QE

New Directions for Testing and Measurement Series
Michael Kean, *Editor-in-Chief*

Contents

Editor's Notes

Generalizability theory brings measurement in psychology and education back to reality. In their influential early writings on generalizability theory, Lee Cronbach and others illustrated realistic perceptions of error variance and procedures to produce credible inferences from test data. The anachronistic formulas of classical theory could be exchanged for dynamic methods that facilitated replicable and representative measurement and that fostered decisions based on measurements that were responsible and utilitarian.

The dynamic nature of generalizability theory is the genesis of this sourcebook. Since generalizability theory was first formulated by Cronbach and his colleagues, its procedures have been expanded and extended to a whole range of measurement and psychometric issues. It appears to be time for the diverse applications of generalizability theory and inference to be presented systematically. The presentation should be intensive enough to represent the various manifestations of generalizability theory yet easy enough to understand that the reader can apply them. This is the goal of this sourcebook: comprehensive presentation of applicable procedures and orientations toward measurement.

This sourcebook is organized to further that goal. Gerald M. Gillmore, Jean Cardinet, and Linda Allal contribute the two introductory chapters. In Chapter One, Gillmore stresses the use of generalizability in program evaluation and decision situations. In Chapter Two, Cardinet and Allal move the reader to conceptualize needs and areas in education for generalization, such as instructional treatments, classrooms, and the like. In Chapter Three, Fyans picks up where Cardinet and Allal leave off. Fyans extends generalizability to redefine validity, particularly external validity, in terms of multilevel research and inference.

Multivariate generalizability deals with the interpretation of a profile or composite of measurements, such as test scores, across several subtests. Chapters Four and Five describe multivariate generalizability in a tractable and articulate fashion. In Chapter Four, Noreen Webb, Richard Shavelson, and Ebrahim Maddahian use data from the Beginning Teacher Evaluation Study to illustrate the differing interpretations of viewing test data from univariate and multivariate perspectives. Their chapter concludes with computer programs that the reader can implement to apply multivariate generalizability. In Chapter Five, Robert Brennan and David Jarjoura use multivariate generalizability techniques to bridge the gap between psychometric constraints and the tables of specifications needed in test development. They illustrate with results from the American College Testing Program.

Due to considerations of length, some material had to be deleted. That material focused primarily on redefining and rethinking validity from a generalizability perspective. Stability of measurement, specifications of the population for which generalizable statements can be made, and decision theory were also addressed. These chapters may appear in a later volume. In any case, their subject matter highlights the breadth and impact of generalizability theory on the measurement community. It is to be hoped that this sourcebook will portray that reality accurately.

I would like to thank the mentors with whom I studied and explored generalizability and measurement theory at the University of Illinois: Robert Linn, Martin Maehr, Maurice Tatsuoka, Harry Triandis, Charles Lewis, and Helen Farmer.

Leslie J. Fyans, Jr.
Editor

Leslie J. Fyans, Jr., is a psychometrician and research psychologist with the testing and assessment program of the Illinois State Board of Education, Springfield. Besides publishing a number of journal articles, he edited Achievement Motivation: Recent Trends in Theory and Research *(Plenum Press, 1980), a comprehensive volume on motivation theory.*

The demands of program evaluation and decision situations are answered through generalizability theory.

Generalizability Theory: Applications to Program Evaluation

Gerald M. Gillmore

The purpose of this chapter is to introduce the unique conceptual framework and language of generalizability theory. Generalizability theory largely supersedes classical test theory by reason of its superior conceptualization and integration. Also, generalizability theory stresses decisions that test measurements support, and it is able to take advantage of complex experimental designs. While this chapter is relevant to any area in which generalizability theory is applicable, it emphasizes evaluation research, and most examples come from that area.

How does generalizability theory relate to experimental design, analysis of variance, and classical test theory? In relation to experimental design, generalizability theory takes advantage of the methodological techniques associated with analysis of variance. Because generalizability theory is commonly applied to situations in which the researcher wishes to discover and quantify individual differences, most designs of interest have subjects as a crossed factor; that is, they make repeated measures on subjects. In contrast, in traditional experimental design applications, subjects are often nested within cells; that is, subjects are treated as replications. Most applications of traditional experimental design use F statistics to test for significance, although many

L. J. Fyans, Jr. (Ed.). *Generalizability Theory: Inferences and Practical Applications.*
New Directions for Testing and Measurement, no. 18. San Francisco: Jossey-Bass, June 1983.

researchers extol strength of association measures (Hays, 1963). For all practical purposes, generalizability theory eschews the use of F tests and concentrates instead on variance component estimates.

In classical test theory, the total observed score variance in a given study is partitioned into two components: true score variance, which is held to reflect true differences among individuals or collections of individuals, and error variance, which is held to reflect undifferentiated random error. The reliability of the measuring instrument is defined as the ratio of true score variance to total observed score variance or to one minus the ratio of error variance to total observed score variance. Unfortunately, true score is often reified, as if it were a thing that the individual being measured possessed independent of the measurement procedure.

In classical test theory, error is assumed to be undifferentiated and univariate, although it often is recognized — explicitly but not operationally — that error can spring from multiple sources. This undifferentiated view of error can lead the quality of the measures to be misperceived. Furthermore, it is possible for the person who wishes to base decisions on data obtained with a measuring device to be working in a context quite dissimilar from that in which the measure's reliability was estimated. In that situation, the true score definition can be inappropriate, and the sources of errors can be different. As a result, the decision maker can accept an estimate of reliability that is inappropriate for the decision to be made. For example, many evaluation studies use results from nationally standardized tests as dependent variables. However, the reliability and validity statistics published by the test's producers are in most cases virtually irrelevant for judging its adequacy for the purpose to which it has been put. This indicates less that the test publisher has failed than that the imprecise and inflexible definitions of true score and error in classical test theory are not well suited to the needs of evaluation research.

The conceptual framework of generalizability theory minimizes these confusions and greatly enhances the amount of information that can be derived from a multifactor study. In generalizability theory, variation in the results of a measurement procedure is partitioned into as many sources as the design of the study allows; often, these sources number more than the two allowed by classical test theory. Which of these multiple sources can appropriately be considered replicable variation (true or universe variance) and of which of these sources can appropriately be considered random error depend on the decision that the data are to inform or support. The definitions can change as the same measurements serve different purposes: for example, to discriminate among individuals or to discriminate among classes of individuals. Roberts's axiom — only errors can exist — is, of course, hyperbole. However, Berman's corollary to Roberts's axiom — one man's error is another man's data — is a central tenet of generalizability theory.

Generalizability Theory

Generalizability theory begins with the recognition that all measurement is fallible or imperfect, but it proceeds to emphasize that error is relative and that error can have multiple sources. One central tenet of generalizability theory is that decision makers inevitably wish to assign meaning to actual measures that in effect generalizes those measures beyond the specific set of conditions used to create them. To make this statement concrete, consider the following: The number of errors that a certain student makes in response to a twenty-item test on multiplication of fractions can be used to assign a grade to the student. But the teacher almost surely thinks that the grade is based on the student's general ability to multiply fractions, an ability that transcends the twenty items, the time of day when the test was given, the item format, and so forth. So put, the measurement question becomes one of generalizability: How well do the values that the concrete procedure has yielded generalize to a more abstract set of conditions of particular interest? As a corollary, to what extent do various theoretically important and controllable factors influence generalizability? For example, it is possible for the time of day when the test was given to have little influence on test scores but for the specific test items chosen to be very influential.

Generalizability and Decision Studies

The conceptual distinction between generalizability (G) studies and decision (D) studies first introduced by Rajaratnam (1960) is basic to an understanding and appreciation of generalizability theory. In essence, a G study is conducted to assess the characteristics of a measuring device. It is performed most effectively in the instrument development stage. In contrast, a D study is a study on which actual decisions will be based. As generalizability analyses are done in support of evaluation research, D study results take on special importance, since they are directly related to the data-based decisions that are to be made. However, a well-conceived and well-conducted G study is crucial to meaningful D study conclusions. The discussion that follows assumes that measurement designs are multifaceted but univariate. Chapters Four and Five in this volume extend the theory to the multivariate case, where scores are treated separately, not as additive members of a composite score.

G Studies

A G study starts with definition of the universe of admissible observations. This concept refers to the factors or variables that the G study takes into consideration and to the range of acceptable conditions for each factor or variable. For example, one factor could be persons, and the universe of admissible observations for persons could be all sixth-grade students in a certain school district. In this case, the actual G study conditions for the persons factor should be a random sample from that universe. Other factors in the G study could be classes and test items. Both factors would also require careful definition of the universe of admissible observations.

The goal of the typical G study is estimation of variance components for all effects that are estimable from the design of the study. Partitioning of the total variance from the study into components that can be attributed to various sources is fundamental to generalizability theory. Consider a relatively simple design in which every person in the sample responds to all the items of a certain test. The design of this study crosses persons with items, which can be denoted $p \times i$. An observed score, denoted Xpi, can be defined as the score of person p on item i. If the items are scored dichotomously — as right or wrong — then Xpi can equal either one or zero for each unique person p and item i. The variance equals .25 if item difficulty equals .5, and it drops as the average departs from .5. For the $p \times i$ design, the total variance of scores can be partitioned into variance due to the item main effect, variance due to the person main effect, and variance due to the person-by-item interaction.

In generalizability theory, the variance component estimates themselves have great importance. Classical test theory partitions variance between two sources, true score variance and error variance. In generalizability theory, a G study yields variance component estimates for all separately estimable effects. These components are susceptible to estimation errors. Cronbach and others (1972) warned of this problem, which Shavelson and Webb (1981, p. 138) neatly placed in perspective: "While we consider the problems associated with estimating variance components to be the Achilles heel of G theory, these problems afflict all sampling theories. One virtue of G theory is that it brings estimation problems to the fore and puts them up for examination." Chapter Three in this volume describes a promising approach to the estimation problem.

D Studies

The general characteristics of the measuring device, whether it is a test, a rating instrument, or something else, are established by a G study. The D study is conducted to assess the characteristics of the measuring device in a particular decision-making context. In most cases, conducting a D study involves collecting new data. A typical and efficient practice in evaluation research is for the G study to be conducted essentially as a pilot test of the instrument with an appropriate random sample. The resulting data can be then used to simulate D study results, but the actual D study conducted to support decision making can involve measurement on a much larger sample — even on an entire population. It is possible for the G and D studies to involve the same data. In either case, the D study definition is dictated by how the data will be interpreted when they are used to make decisions. The D study definition can be viewed as the result of four decisions. That is, the decision maker must specify the object of measurement, the universe of generalization, the number of conditions to be sampled from each facet, and the experimental design.

The Object of Measurement. The object of measurement for a D study is the G study factor about which decisions are to be made. The object of measurement is often persons, but other objects are also possible. In a design that nests persons within classes and crosses persons with item, the object of measurement is appropriately classes if the purpose of the measurement is to make judgments about classes.

Considerations relating to the definition of the object of measurement are particularly important in evaluation research, because the object of measurement is often something other than persons. Kane and Brennan (1977) cite evaluations of Head Start and Follow Through as examples of evaluations in which class is the appropriate object of measurement. Presenting findings from the evaluation of Follow Through, Kennedy (1978, p. 3) pointed out that "Several levels of data aggregation were considered as units of analysis: the child, the classroom, the school building, and the community (the site)." Research on student instructional ratings has included generalizability studies in which the class, the teacher, and the course have all been objects of measurement (Gillmore and others, 1978; Kane and others, 1976; Smith, 1979). Chapter Two in this volume indicates how generalizability procedures can be used with data at various levels of data aggregation and inference.

To emphasize that successive objects of measurement can be studied within the same design, Cardinet and others (1976, 1981) introduced the principle of symmetry." The principle of symmetry of the data is simply an affirmation that each factor of a design can be selected as an object of study and that G study operations designed for one factor can be transposed in the study of other factors" (Cardinet and others, 1981, p. 184). These authors use the expressions *face of differentiation* to refer to facets corresponding to objects of measurement and *face of instrumentation* to refer to conditions of measurement.

The Universe of Generalization. If one single concept lies at the heart of generalizability theory, it is the concept of the universe of generalization and the closely related concept of the universe of admissible observations. The universe of admissible observations refers to the factors that one chooses systematically to take into consideration in the G study and to the range of conditions that can be sampled from each. Facet denotes factors included in the D study that are not the object of measurement. For example, if the factors of the study are persons and items and the object of measurement for the D study is persons, then the items factor is a facet of the D study. To use the terminology of Cardinet and others (1981), persons constitutes the face of differentiation in this example and items constitutes the face of instrumentation.

The universe of generalization for a given D study is closely related to the universe of admissible observation defined in the G study, in that the former cannot be larger in any respect than the latter. That is, the D study cannot include facets not present as factors in the G study, and it cannot define the universe of generalization for a facet that is not completely contained in the corresponding universe of admissible observations of the G study. However, the former can be a subset of the latter. For example, factors of the G study for which the associated variance components are negligible can be collapsed and not defined as facets of the D study.

The issue at stake in determining the universe of generalization is the set of conditions to which the decision maker wishes to generalize the resulting measures. In defining this set of conditions, each facet can be considered in one of three ways, depending on the universe to which the decision maker wishes to generalize the results. First, the conditions of a facet can be assumed to be a random sample from an essentially infinite set of possible admissible conditions. This assumption is justifiable if the decision maker wishes to generalize to the entire set. For example, a random sample of sites could be selected for trial implementation of a compensatory education program, with sites being one of the facets of the D study. However, the entire set of possible sites at which the program could be implemented can be considered as lying within the universe of generalization. Thus, results can be generalized to the entire set of sites. Consistent with conventions in the literature on analysis of variance, facets considered in this way are termed *random*. Second, the conditions of a facet can be assumed to exhaust the entire set of admissible conditions for that facet. In this case, generalization beyond the set is not of interest. To return to the example just cited, only the sites used in the D study could be defined as lying within the universe of generalization for the sites facet. Facets considered in this way are termed *fixed*. Third, the decision maker may wish to generalize the results to a set of conditions for a facet that is larger than the set sampled in the D study but still not infinite. For example, twenty states could be chosen at random for a trial of a statewide program. However, the decision makers could wish to generalize the results to all fifty states. In such a case, generalization is intended to be to a finite universe. This case is unusual in generalizability theory. In this chapter, attention will be restricted to fixed and random universes of generalization.

The Number of Conditions for Each Facet. In the G study, a certain number of conditions or levels are sampled for each factor in order to estimate the variance components for each effect of the design. However, the number of conditions sampled for each facet in the D study is not restricted to the sample sizes of the G study. Rather, that number must be specified by the decision maker. Indeed, an investigator can vary the number of conditions that can be sampled in the D study systematically in order to forecast the resulting dependability. For example, using the person-by-items design, if a G study is conducted with fifty items, the number of levels for that factor will be fifty. But, if the decision maker wants to base judgments on a test of only twenty items, the number of conditions for the item facet in the D study will be twenty, not fifty.

The G study variance component estimates are based on a single average level for each effect. For the D study, the variance component estimate associated with a given effect is divided by the number of conditions of the effect over which a score is averaged within the object of measurement. In other words, the D study variance component estimate for a given effect is equal to the corresponding G study variance component estimate divided by the number of D study conditions for that effect within the object of measurement. G study and D study variance component estimates are equal for effects that contain only the object of measurement. Table 1 depicts the G study variance component estimates and the comparable D study variance component estimates for the $(p{:}c) \times i$ design, assuming that classes are the object of measurement and that the design is balanced. The number of items in the D study is denoted by n'_i, and the number of persons within each class is denoted by n'_p. The primes are included to denote the number of D study conditions.

The reader will notice that the variance component estimate for the class main effect in Table 1 is not altered from the G study to the D study, since it contains only the object of measurement. The variance component estimate for the classes-by-item interaction is divided by the number of items in the D study. The persons-by-items-within-classes effect $(pi{:}c)$ is divided by both the number of items and the number of persons, since the effect (person's performance) contains both facets and the product of the number of conditions of the two that are sampled within the object of measurement.

A G study design can differ from a D study design by the design of the latter excluding factors of the former. For example, the age of the rater could be a factor of the G study, but in the D study all raters could be chosen to have the same age, or rater age could be allowed to vary, and no attention could be

Table 1. G Study and D Study Variance Components for the $(p{:}c) \times i$ Design with Classes as the Object of Measurement

Effects	G Study Variance Component	D Study Variance Component
c	$\sigma^2(c)$	$\sigma^2(c)$
$p{:}c$	$\sigma^2(p{:}c)$	$\sigma^2(p{:}c)/n'_p$
i	$\sigma^2(i)$	$\sigma^2(i)/n'_i$
ci	$\sigma^2(ci)$	$\sigma^2(ci)/n'_i$
$pi{:}c$	$\sigma^2(pi{:}c)$	$\sigma^2(pi{:}c)/(n'_p n'_i)$

c = classes
p = persons
i = items
$:$ = nested within

paid to it. Again, this change of design may be imposed by resource limitations, but it should be informed by G study results. All variance component estimates associated with the rater age factor could be of negligible magnitude and thus of little consequence in determining the outcomes of the measurements. However, if the estimates were large, it could suggest that the age facet cannot be left to vary randomly without serious consequences.

The Experimental Design. Often, the experimental design for the D study is identical to the experimental design of the G study. Two exceptions come immediately to mind. First, a factor crossed with other factors in the G study can become a nested factor in the D study. A good example of this is a task requiring judgments by raters, such as grading the written essays of persons. In the G study, all raters could rate all items on all essays. This would allow independent estimates to be made of the variance components due to raters, to persons, and to the raters-by-persons interaction. In the D study, essays could be nested within raters; thus, rater one could rate the first twenty essays, rater two the next twenty, and so on. The reader should note that, in both examples in which the D study design differs from the G study design, the D study is a subset of the G study. To repeat, a D study cannot treat a facet or the object of measurement as crossed when it is nested in the G study, nor can a D study include facets that are not factors in the G study. Otherwise, all the variance component estimates necessary for D study inferences would not be available from the G study.

D Study Indices of Dependability

Certain statistics based on D study variance component estimates can be useful in assessing the measuring device, especially as indices of dependability. In essence, indices of dependability are squared correlations between universe and observed scores. The precise definition varies with the definitions of universe and observed score. Operationally, dependability is defined as the ratio of universe score variance to the sum of universe score variance and error variance. When decisions are made on a comparative basis, the appropriate error is δ, and the denominator of the index of dependability is the expected observed score variance. In this case, the index is termed the *generalizability coefficient*, and it is denoted by ϵp^2. When decisions are made on an absolute basis, the appropriate error is Δ, and the generalizability coefficient is likely to overestimate dependability. The dependability index that is appropriate when decisions are made on an absolute basis will be discussed in the next section. Also discussed in the next section are the two error indices, δ and Δ, as used with norm-referenced and domain-referenced tests, respectively.

The generalizability coefficient, ϵp^2, is analogous to the reliability coefficient in classical test theory. In classical test theory, reliability is defined as the ratio of true score variance to observed score variance. In generalizability theory, dependability is defined as the ratio of universe score variance to expected observed score variance. "It is completely comparable to the traditional reliability coefficient except that full attention has to be given to the universe definition and to the design of the D study" (Cronbach and others, 1972, p. 97).

The generalizability coefficient is an intraclass correlation that can be interpreted as an average correlation over the objects of measurement among successive replications of the D study design. Each replication uses the same objects of measurement (for example, the same person), the same conditions for fixed facets, and a new, same-size random sample of conditions for random facets. The scores theoretically correlated are deviations from the overall mean for each replication. The generalizability coefficient can also be viewed as an approximation of the squared correlation between the observed deviation scores and the universe deviation scores.

For the $(p{:}c) \times i$ design with classes as the object of measurement, there are four possible generalizability coefficients, depending on whether the items facet is treated as fixed or random and on whether the persons facet is treated as fixed or random. When both items and persons are treated as fixed facets, the generalizability coefficient is a trivial 1.0, since there is no independent estimate of error variance, and thus the estimate for universe score variance is the same as the estimate for the expected observed score variance. The formulas corresponding to the remaining possibilities follow. (For clarity, the facets of the D study are placed in parentheses after the $\epsilon\rho^2$; an asterisk denotes a fixed facet.) $\hat{\epsilon}\sigma^2(x)$ is the expected observed score variance.

Persons random, items random:

$$(1) \qquad \hat{\epsilon}\rho^2(P,I) = \hat{\sigma}^2(c)/\hat{\epsilon}\sigma^2(x)$$

Persons random, items fixed:

$$(2) \qquad \hat{\epsilon}\rho^2(P,I^*) = [\hat{\sigma}^2(c) + \hat{\sigma}^2(ci)/n'_i]/\hat{\epsilon}\sigma^2(x)$$

Persons fixed, items random:

$$(3) \qquad \hat{\epsilon}\rho^2(P^*,I) = [\hat{\sigma}^2(c) + \hat{\sigma}^2(p{:}c)/n'_p]/\hat{\epsilon}\sigma^2(x)$$

For this particular design, $\hat{\epsilon}\rho^2(P,I^*)$ is essentially equivalent to inter-rater reliability in classical test theory (Ebel, 1951). Similarly, $\hat{\epsilon}\rho^2(P^*,I)$ is essentially equivalent to interitem reliability or internal consistency (Cronbach, 1951). There is no counterpart of $\hat{\epsilon}\rho^2(P,I)$ in classical test theory.

The Testing of Persons

Testing programs represent a major source of data for educational and evaluative research and decision making. Although achievement tests are sometimes used to evaluate teachers, programs, and even the success of school desegregation efforts (Bradley and Bradley, 1977), in the main tests are intended to evaluate the persons to whom they are administered, and that is the function of achievement tests that this section addresses. However, the discussion could easily be extended to decision-making contexts in which an object of measurement other than persons was appropriate.

In the recent literature, distinctions are drawn between norm-referenced tests and domain or criterion-referenced tests (Hambleton and others, 1978). There are reasonably clear differences in the purposes that these two types of test serve and in how they are constructed. The goal of norm-referenced tests is discrimination among examinees. Hence, norm-referenced tests are developed to maximize the variance of test scores. The items of norm-referenced tests tend to be relatively general in nature. In contrast, domain-referenced tests are designed to assess specific competencies. The assessment of individual differences is of minor importance, and individual items are specifically tied to desired behaviors or skills. Following Brennan and Kane (1977a), we will term a domain-referenced test with a single absolute cutting score that defines successful performance a *mastery test*. Licensing examinations and minimum competency examinations are mastery tests.

It is important to recognize that these two types of test differ not only in their characteristics but also in the interpretation of their results. There are at least two distinct ways in which test scores can be interpreted. First, an individual's score averaged over the set of items of a given test can be related to the average score of other persons who took the test at the same time or who took it previously as a norm group. A test interpreted in this way is a norm-referenced test. Second, an individual's score can be related only to the item domain itself, not to how others have performed on the same test. The standards in this case are relative to the item domain, and a test interpreted in this way is a domain-referenced test. Thus, a mastery test is a domain-referenced test interpreted in relation to a single cutoff score, and that cutoff score is chosen with regard to the item domain, not with regard to the performance of a norm group.

Confusion is caused by the fact that results from the same test can be given either a domain- or norm-referenced interpretation, although a single test probably does not fulfill both functions equally well. Thus, it is not quite proper to speak of norm-referenced and domain referenced tests. However, the literature on this area seems to be content to do so, and I follow its lead here. The reader should keep in mind, however, that the fundamental distinction rests on how the test is to be interpreted.

To illustrate the approach of generalizability theory to these three types of test, the design that crosses persons with items $(p \times i)$ will be used. The illustration applies to more complex designs as well, including persons nested with items, items nested within subtests, and subtests nested within tests. The development that follows can easily be extended to these more complex designs (Brennan, 1978). Chapter Five in this volume is relevant in that regard. The G study conducted using the $p \times i$ design yields three variance component estimates: $\hat{\sigma}^2(p)$, $\hat{\sigma}^2(i)$, and $\hat{\sigma}^2(pi)$. For the purposes of illustration, I will assume that the object of measurement is persons, as it is in almost any application of this design. Cardinet and others (1976, 1981) have suggested applications in which items are the object of measurement.

With persons as the object of measurement, the items factor is the only facet of the study; it will be considered as random throughout this discussion. When the items facet is treated as random, the items used in the G study are assumed to be a random sample from some well-defined universe or domain of items, and the items used in the D study are assumed to be a random sample from the same domain. Clearly, the item domain must be meaningful if generalization is to have any meaning. If the domain is a hodgepodge of items the average over which does not measure any unitary ability, then assessment of the test's dependability has little value. An index of dependability is meaningful only insofar as the universe of generalization—in this case, the item domain—is meaningful, whether scores are to be interpreted relative to the item domain or to other scores and, in the former case, whether there is a single cutoff score of interest or not.

Norm-Referenced Tests. What is of interest in norm-referenced tests is not an individual's absolute score but the relation between the individual's score and the scores of others. Thus, the proper error variance to use in this context is the error variance for making comparative judgments, $\sigma^2(\delta)$. For the D study design that we are considering, the variance component associated with the persons-by-items interaction is the only relevant statistic. The proper index of dependability is the generalizability coefficient, which is defined as the universe score variance—in this case, the variance component associated with the persons effect—divided by the expected observed score variance:

$$(4) \qquad \hat{\epsilon}\rho^2(I) = \hat{\sigma}^2(p)/[\hat{\sigma}^2(p) + \hat{\sigma}^2(pi)/n_i']$$

For the $p \times i$ design with persons as the object of measurement and the items facet treated as random, $\epsilon\rho^2(I)$ is equivalent to KR-20 (Kuder and Richardson, 1937) for dichotomously scored items and to Cronbach's alpha (Cronbach, 1951) in the more general case. Furthermore, the magnitude of $\epsilon\rho^2(I)$ alters as a function of the number of D study items on which decisions will be based, exactly as it does in applications of the Spearman-Brown formula. In general, the Spearman–Brown formula holds only in situations where there is no more than one random facet.

It is especially important to note that the variance component estimate associated with the item main effect is not a source of error variance for making comparative decisions. Such decisions are based on the score of each individual averaged over all items. Thus, differences in item difficulty do not affect the deviation score for each individual.

Domain-Referenced Tests. In this section, we will discuss only the general case in which there is no particular cutoff score of interest and in which interpretations are related to the item domain, not to the performance of others. We will discuss mastery interpretations in the section that follows.

The universe score variance for domain-referenced tests is defined in the same way as it is for norm-referenced tests. For the $p \times i$ design, the universe score is estimated by the variance component associated with the main effect of persons, as already noted. However, the proper error variance for this interpretation is the error variance within the object of measurement, $\sigma^2(\Delta)$ (Brennan and Kane, 1977a). The error variance within the object of measurement differs from the expected error variance for making comparative judgments in that the former includes all variance component estimates containing a random facet index, while the latter includes only those variance component estimates containing both a random facet index and the object of measurement index. For the $p \times i$ design, the error variance within the object of measurement is estimated as follows:

$$(5) \qquad \hat{\sigma}^2(\Delta) = \hat{\sigma}^2(i)/n_i' + \hat{\sigma}^2(pi)/n_i'$$

For this design, the difference between $\hat{\sigma}^2(\delta)$ and $\hat{\sigma}^2(\Delta)$ is that the latter includes the term $\hat{\sigma}(i)/n_i'$. Intuitively, the reason for this is that judgments about individuals' abilities are based on the scores of these individuals on a set of items that represents a particular random sample from the item domain. Individuals' scores would be expected to change as different sets of items from the same domain were chosen at random. Under a norm-referenced interpretation, such changes are unimportant, because individual's relative positions do not change. But, under a domain-referenced interpretation, such changes can be important. If all items were equally difficult, the particular items chosen would not influence persons' absolute scores, $\hat{\sigma}^2(i)$ would equal zero, and $\hat{\sigma}^2(\delta)$ would equal $\hat{\sigma}^2(\Delta)$. Otherwise, $\hat{\sigma}^2(\Delta)$ will be larger than $\hat{\sigma}^2(\delta)$, because the specific set of items chosen influences individuals' absolute scores, and the error variance increases as a result.

The index of dependability for domain-referenced tests, then, is the ratio of universe score variance to the sum of universe score variance and error variance within the object of measurement. The denominator for this index is generally not equal to the expected observed score variance; hence, it is not a generalizability coefficient as defined in this chapter. Following Brennan (1978), I will use the generic label *index of dependability* here; it is denoted by Φ. For the $p \times i$ design, the index of dependability for domain-referenced tests is estimated as follows:

$$(6) \qquad \hat{\Phi} = \hat{\sigma}^2(p)/[\hat{\sigma}^2(p) + \hat{\sigma}^2(i)/n_i' + \hat{\sigma}^2(pi)/n_i']$$

Mastery Tests. A mastery test is a domain-referenced test that has a single cutting score. Individuals who match or exceed this score are said to have mastered the content represented by the item domain. Individuals who score below the mastery level are said to have failed to master the content. The discussion of the dependability of mastery tests that follows takes the generalizability theory perspective, which bases error on the differences between observed and universe absolute scores. An alternative and more popular approach is to view errors as misclassifications and to use Cohen's $\varkappa$ or some variant as an index of reliability (Hambleton and others, 1978).

The proper error term for the index of dependability remains the error variance within the object of measurement, as in the general case of domain-referenced interpretations. However, interest is now focused on the individual's absolute performance in relation to a cutting score, denoted by λ. As a result, a term that reflects the difference between the mean of the test and the cutting score must be added to both the numerator and the denominator of the formula for the dependability index. If the population mean is denoted by μ and the cutoff score by λ, the formula for the dependability of mastery tests is as follows (Brennan, 1978):

$$(7) \qquad \Phi(\lambda) = [\sigma^2(p) + (\mu - \lambda)^2] / [\sigma^2(p) + \sigma^2(i)/n'_i + \sigma^2(pi)/n'_i + (\mu - \lambda)^2]$$

The formula for the estimation of $\Phi(\lambda)$ is somewhat complicated, because simply substituting the sample mean for μ leads to a biased estimate of the squared difference between the population mean and the cutoff score (Brennan and Kane, 1977a, 1977b).

If $\lambda - \mathbf{M}$, the index of dependability for mastery tests is equivalent to the index of dependability for domain-referenced tests that have no particular cutoff score. Otherwise, the dependability of the test for making mastery decisions improves as λ departs from μ. The most difficult situation for mastery decisions is when individuals' scores cluster around the cutoff score. The easiest situation is when individuals' scores cluster elsewhere.

References

Bradley, L. A., and Bradley, G. W. "The Academic Achievement of Black Students in Desegregated Schools: A Critical Review." *Review of Educational Research,* 1977, *47,* 399–449.

Brennan, R. L. *Extensions of Generalizability Theory to Domain-Referenced Testing.* ACT Technical Bulletin, No. 30. Iowa City: American College Testing Program, 1978.

Brennan, R. L., and Kane, M. T. "An Index of Dependability for Mastery Tests." *Journal of Educational Measurement,* 1977a, *14,* 277–289.

Brennan, R. L., and Kane, M. T. "Signal/Noise Ratios for Domain-Referenced Tests." *Psychometrika,* 1977, *42,* 91–92.

Cardinet, J., Tourneur, Y., and Allal, L. "The Symmetry of Generalizability Theory Applications to Educational Measurement." *Journal of Educational Measurement,* 1976, *13,* 119–135.

Cardinet, J., Tourneur, Y., and Allal, L. "Extension of Generalizability Theory and Its Applications in Educational Measurement." *Journal of Educational Measurement,* 1981, *18,* 183–204.

Cronbach, L. J. "Coefficient Alpha and the Internal Structure of Tests." *Psychometrika,* 1951, *16,* 297–334.

Cronbach, L. J., Gleser, G. C., Nanda, H., and Rajaratnam, N. *The Dependability of Behavioral Measurements: Theory of Generalizability for Scores and Profiles.* New York: Wiley, 1972.

Cronbach, L. J., Rajaratnam, N., and Gleser, G. C. "Theory of Generalizability: A Liberalization of Reliability Theory." *British Journal of Mathematical and Statistical Psychology,* 1963, *16,* 137–163.

Ebel, R. L. "Estimation of the Reliability of Ratings." *Psychometrika,* 1951, *16,* 407–424.

Gillmore, G. M., Kane, M. T., and Naccarato, R. W. "The Generalizability of Student Ratings of Instruction: Estimation of the Teacher and Course Components." *Journal of Educational Measurement,* 1978, *15,* 1–13.

Hambleton, R. K., Swaminathan, H., Algina, J., and Coulson, D. B. "Criterion-Referenced Testing and Measurement: A Review of Technical Issues and Developments." *Review of Educational Research,* 1978, *48,* 1–48.

Hays, W. L. *Statistics for Psychologists.* New York: Holt, Rinehart and Winston, 1963.

Kane, M. T., and Brennan, R. L. *Agreement Coefficients as Indices of Dependability for Domain-Referenced Tests.* ACT Technical Bulletin, No. 28. Iowa City: American College Testing Program, 1977.

Kane, M. T., Gillmore, G. M., and Crooks, T. J. "Student Evaluations of Teaching: The Generalizability of Class Means." *Journal of Educational Measurement,* 1976, *13,* 171–184.

Kennedy, M. M. "Findings from the Follow Through Planned Variation Study." *Educational Researcher,* 1978, *7,* 3–11.

Kuder, G. R., and Richardson, M. W. "The Theory of the Estimation of Test Reliability." *Psychometrika,* 1937, *2,* 151–160.

Rajaratnam, N. "Reliability Formulas for Independent Decision Data When Data Are Matched." *Psychometrika,* 1960, *25,* 261–271.

Shavelson, R. L., and Webb, N. M. "Generalizability Theory: 1973–1980." *British Journal of Mathematical and Statistical Psychology,* 1981, *34,* 133–166.

Smith, P. L. "The Generalizability of Student Ratings of Courses: Asking the Right Questions." *Journal of Educational Measurement,* 1979, *16,* 77–88.

Note. This chapter represents an abridgement of a more complete paper which may be obtained from the author.

Gerald M. Gillmore is director of the Educational Assessment Center and associate professor of psychology at the University of Washington.

A wide range of measurement situations requiring generalizability of factors, such as instructional objectives, classrooms, treatment, and stages of learning, are of interest to researchers in behavioral sciences.

Estimation of Generalizability Parameters

Jean Cardinet
Linda Allal

This chapter presents a general framework for conducting generalizability analyses. This framework permits generalizability parameters to be estimated for a wide range of measurement designs of interest to researchers in the behavioral sciences. It incorporates a series of general algorithms applicable to any complete factorial design formed by crossed factors, nested factors, or both, providing that the number of observations is the same in each cell of the design. The calculation procedures take into account multiple sources of variation not only in the estimation of error variance but also in the estimation of the true variance due to characteristics of the objects of measurement.

The procedures described in this chapter permit generalizability analysis to be extended to types of designs not dealt with previously, in particular to designs in which the objects of study are a random sample from a finite population or in which they are fixed. For these cases, it is necessary to introduce an adjustment algorithm in order to use the estimates of mixed model variance components defined by Cornfield and Tukey (1956) for the estimation of generalizability parameters, as defined by the model of Cronbach and others (1963). The framework also incorporates several algorithms developed by Brennan (1983), but it presents them in a somewhat different theoretical perspective.

L. J. Fyans, Jr. (Ed.). *Generalizability Theory: Inferences and Practical Applications.*
New Directions for Testing and Measurement, no. 18. San Francisco: Jossey-Bass, June 1983.

The formulation of an enlarged framework for generalizability analysis entails a certain number of new concepts and a new terminology described in detail by Cardinet and others (1981, 1982). This chapter begins with a rapid overview of the framework. Then, it focuses on the calculation procedures — algorithms and corresponding diagrams — used in each phase of a generalizability analysis. The authors assume that the reader is familiar with the basic concepts of analysis of variance.

Limits of Existing Formulation

There may be several reasons why the important publication of Cronbach and others (1972) has had less scientific impact than it deserves. One reason is that the authors tend to focus on psychometric applications of generalizability theory aimed at the study of individual differences. This tendency is illustrated by their assumption that the persons factor in a design is the object of study. Thus, the term *facet* is applied only to the other design factors corresponding to the conditions of observation. However, this restriction is not necessary. The principles of generalizability theory can easily be extended to other objects of measurement.

A second reason is that there is some confusion in the presentation of the roles of analysis of variance and of generalizability theory. Two examples of this confusion can be mentioned. First, although the estimation of variance components is often presented as the essential aspect of a generalizability study, this is in fact solely an outcome of analysis of variance. Second, in designs that involve fixed conditions along a facet of observation, the interaction between persons and this facet is treated as a component of true (universe score) variance. Strictly speaking, such interaction does not affect the variance of the observed scores; that is, the sum of the interaction effects is zero for each person. A better justification for the procedure proposed by Cronbach and others is that the variance component for persons is estimated differently under the mixed model and under the purely random model of analysis of variance. Again, an aspect of analysis of variance needs to be distinguished from issues of measurement.

A third reason lies in the fact that the authors deal with the choice of the object of study implicitly. Explication of this choice in in fact essential to the application of concepts of measurement. In a situation of curriculum evaluation, for example, the objects of study are the achievement levels attained for different items, not the achievement levels attained by different persons. Although this transposition has no effect on the results of the analysis of variance, it completely transforms the generalizability study by reversing the sources of true variance and error variance. The essential feature of a generalizability analysis is a consequence of the choice of the objects of study, not of the estimation of variance components.

The Four Phases of Generalizability Analysis

In the framework that we propose, the term *facet* is applied to all factors present in the design used for data collection. The first two phases of analysis are based on the analysis of variance model, and the last two phases are based on concepts specific to the model of generalizability theory. Figure 1 is an overview of the four phases of analysis. For each phase, it indicates the underlying model, the types of information taken into consideration, the corresponding calculation procedures, and the results obtained. The four phases entail increasingly precise specification of the design leading to a choice in the final phase of the best design for future research and decision making. It should be pointed out that the sequence of the four phases corresponds to the order in which analysis and estimation procedures are applied once the data have been collected; it does not imply that conceptual issues are dealt with in this order when data collection is being planned. Substantive questions, such as choice of the object of study, must be considered first, even if the consequences of this choice do not affect the initial phases of analysis.

Phase One. The observation design describes the structure of the data set that has been collected: the facets considered, the relationships (crossing, nesting) among facets, the number of observed levels of each facet. It permits all sources of variation under consideration to be specified, as well as sources of variation that are confounded. By applying the usual analysis of variance equations for analysis of the sums of squares, one obtains the observed mean squares for each source of variation.

Phase Two. The estimation design specifies the type of population (infinite, finite) from which the levels of each facet are selected and the mode of sampling employed. If the number of admissible levels (N) is larger than the number of observed levels (n), we can assume that the latter have been randomly sampled. The estimation design introduces a distinction among the facets formed by three modes of sampling: random sampling from an infinite population, random sampling from a finite population $(N > n)$, and exhaustive selection of all levels of a finite population $(N = n)$. The definitions and hypotheses of Cornfield and Tukey (1956) can be used to estimate the variance components of the appropriate random or mixed model defined in this phase.

Phase Three. The measurement design distinguishes the objects of study from the conditions of observation. The objects of study are defined by the facets of differentiation, which together constitute the face of differentiation of the design (**D** face). The conditions of observation are defined by the facets of instrumentation, which constitute the face of instrumentation of the design (**I** face). The distinction between the **D** face and the **I** face of the measurement design implies specification of the population of admissible objects of study (formed by the combination of all admissible levels of the differentiation facets) and of the universe of admissible conditions of observation (formed by

Figure 1. Framework for Conducting Generalizability Analyses

Model	Phase	Information regarding the facets	Type of design	Result of calculations	Symbols	Steps in carrying out the calculations
ANALYSIS OF VARIANCE	1	Identification - choice of facets - relationships among facets (crossed, nested, confounded) - number of observed levels (per facet) *Specifies the set of observed data*	Observation	Mean squares	α $MS(\alpha)$	1 Source of variation : Identify the sources corresponding to all main effect and interaction effects. The total subscript of an effect (α) is noted as follows: (primary subscript(s)) : (1st nesting subscript(s)) : ... : (nth nesting subscript(s)), e.g. (ip:c:s) for the interaction of items with pupils nested in classes nested in schools. 2 Mean squares : Compute the mean square for each effect (α). (See Millman and Glass, 1967).
	2	Sampling Number of admissible levels and mode of sampling determine whether a facet is : . purely random . finite random . fixed *Specifies the domain of admissible observations*	Estimation	Variance components, random or mixed model	$\hat{\sigma}^2(\alpha)$ $\hat{\sigma}^2(\alpha\|M)$	3 Random model variance components : For each effect (α) comput[e] $$MS(\alpha) + \sum_{i=1}^{i=j} (-1)^i \left(\begin{array}{l} \text{sum of the mean squares whose total subscripts} \\ \text{contain } \alpha \text{ plus the letter(s) for i additional} \\ \text{facet(s), each of which appeared in subscripts} \\ \text{at step (i - 1) for i > 1} \end{array} \right)$$ where (i) is the rank (from 1 to j) of the expression between parentheses (} and (j) is the number of such expressions. Divide this expression by f(α), the product of the numbers of observed levels of all facets not appearing in the total subscript of the effect (α). 4 Mixed model variance components : For a design with one or more fixed and/or finite facets, the mixed model estimate is: $$\hat{\sigma}^2(\alpha\|M) = \hat{\sigma}^2(\alpha) + \sum_j \frac{\hat{\sigma}^2(\beta_j)}{f(\beta_j)}, \text{ where}$$ $\hat{\sigma}^2(\beta_j)$ = random model estimates of all other components, which include all letters of the component (α) in their total subscript $f(\beta_j)$ = product of the numbers of admissible levels of the facets appearing in the subscript of β_j but not in the subscript (α) Carry out subsequent calculations using the components obtained in this step

	Role in measurement		Component	Symbol	Procedure

3	**Role in measurement**
	
	- Differentiation face: D facets
	  • random D facets: D^R
	  • fixed D facets: D^F
	- Instrumentation face: I facets
	  • random I facets: I^R
	  • fixed I facets: I^F
	
	Specifies the population of admissible objects of measurement and the universe of admissible conditions of measurement
		Mea-
		su-
		re-
		ment
			Allocation of the facets of the measurement design and specification of the active variance components	$M(D^R/D^F/I^F/I^R)$	5 Measurement design(s) : Define one or more design(s) to be analysed by steps 6 through 12.

					6 Control of coherence : Verify that there are no D facets nested within I facets, confoundind D-variance and error.
					7 Active variance : Eliminate components having I^F facet(s) in their primary subscript.
					8 Expectancies of variance : Multiply components by $(N_f-1)/N_f$ for each fixed or finite facet in their primary subscript.
			Differentiation variance	$\hat{\sigma}^2(\tau)$	9 Differentiation variance : Extract from the active variance and sum all components which include only D facets in their primary subscript.
			Error (generalization) variances	$\hat{\sigma}^2(\Delta)$	10 Absolute error variance : Sum all the remaining components, each weighted by $(1/n_i)$ for each I facet in its total subsc. & by $(N_i-n_i)/(N_i n_i)$ for each finite I facet in its primary subsc.
				$\hat{\sigma}^2(\delta)$	11 Relative error variance : Extract from the preceding expression and sum with their coefficients all components which include at least one D facet in their total subscript.
			Generalizability coefficient	$\hat{E}\rho^2$	12 Generalizability coefficient(s) : Divide the differentiation variance by the sum of the differentiation variance and the error variance under consideration $(\hat{\sigma}^2(\delta), \hat{\sigma}^2(\Delta))$.
4	**Modifications** - Relationship among facets (nesting or confounding of previously crossed facets) - Number of observed levels (increased levels for I^R facets) - Number and mode of sampling of admissible levels of D or I facets *Specifies the recommended population(s) of differentiation and universe(s) of generalization*	Op- ti- mi- za- tion	Allocation of facets of optimization design and specification of active variance components	$O(D^R/D^F/I^F/I^R)$	13 Optimization design(s) : Define one or more design(s) taking into consideration modifications of the initial observation, estimation and measurement designs, in order to decrease error, to improve validity, or to decrease costs. Repeat, as appropriate, steps 3 to 8.
			Differentiation variance	$\hat{\sigma}^2(\tau')$	14 Differentiation variance : Repeat step 9.
			Error (generalization) variances	$\hat{\sigma}^2(\Delta')$ $\hat{\sigma}^2(\delta')$	15 Error variances : Repeat steps 10 and 11.
			Generalizability coefficient	$\hat{E}\rho^2$	16 Generalizability coefficient(s) : Repeat step 12.

the combination of all admissible levels of the instrumentation facets). Next, the definitions and rules of generalizability theory are applied to estimate three parameters: the variance of the universe scores (variance of differentiation), the variance of absolute measurement error, and the variance of relative measurement error. Generalizability coefficients can then be calculated from these estimates.

Phase Four. The results of phase three are used to define the optimization design in phase four. Defining the optimization design entails specification of one or more modified designs permitting more precise estimation of the valid differentiation variance, reduction of error variance, or decrease of the cost of data collection. The calculation algorithms of this phase are essentially the same as those of the preceding phases, except that they are applied to the designs that replace the designs defined previously. The operations in phase four correspond approximately to those of the decision study described by Cronbach and others (1972), but they take into consideration aims of measurement in any type of research, not just in the context of decision making.

The Framework Illustrated

The framework that we propose can be illustrated by a concrete application that demonstrates the calculation procedures presented in Figure 1 step by step. The application that we use (Pilliner, 1965, p. 65) is already classic, since it has been used by Cronbach and others (1972, p. 226) to illustrate generalizability calculations.

Pilliner carried out an analysis of variance on the performance of twenty-eight students on an arithmetic test composed of seventy-five questions nested within three strata; there were twenty-five questions per stratum. The results of Pilliner's analysis are displayed in Table 1. Table 1 corresponds to the outcome of the first phase of our framework. The formulas for this phase and for the subsequent phases will be presented in detail in the context of this example.

Calculation Procedures for Phase One

Notation. For each source of variation, there is a corresponding variance component: $\sigma^2(\alpha)$. A component is identified by placing the initials of the facets involved between parentheses after the symbol σ^2. For a nonnested main effect the subscript includes a single initial—for example, $\sigma^2(p)$ for persons. For interaction effects, the subscript contains a series of adjacent initials—for example, $\sigma^2(ps)$ for persons crossed with strata. A colon indicates relationships of nesting between facets. For example, $(a{:}b)$ signifies that facet a is nested in facet b. If there are several successive levels of nesting—for example, if pupils are nested in classes, which are nested in schools—the relationships are symbolized by a series of colons—for example, $\sigma^2(p{:}c{:}e)$. For the Pilliner example,

Table 1. Analysis of Variance from the Study by Pilliner (1965)

Source of Variation	Sum of Squares	df	Mean Square
Persons *(P)*	100.1471	27	3.7092
Strata *(S)*	4.2137	2	2.1066
Questions *(Q:S)*	97.5585	72	1.3550
Persons × Strata *(PS)*	12.5374	54	0.2322
Persons × Questions *(PQ:S)*	305.6811	1944	0.1572
Total	520.1378	2099	

the variance component for questions nested in strata is designated by $\sigma^2(q{:}s)$. The notation of the variance component for the interaction of persons with questions nested in strata is symbolized by *(pq:s)*. The primary subscript of a variance component is composed of the letters appearing to the left of the first colon in the total subscript—for example *pq* in the subscript *(pq:s)*. The number of observed levels of each facet is indicated by n with the initial of the facet in subscript—for example, number of persons by n_p, number of strata by n_s.

Identification of the Variance Components. In a fully crossed design, there is a source of variation for each facet (that is, for each main effect) and for each interaction due to the combination of two, three, four, or more facets (that is, for each interaction effect). For a design with x facets, a total of $x + (2^x - x - 1)$ potential sources of variation can be identified by taking all combinations of the initials used to designate the facets. In the Pilliner example, the main effects are *(p)*, *(s)*, and *(q:s)*, and the interaction effects are *(ps)*, *(pq:s)*, *(sq:s)*, and *(psq:s)*.

When a design includes nested facets, it is not possible to estimate a variance component for the interactions between the facets involved in a nesting relationship. These sources of variation can be identified by the fact that the same letter appears on both sides of the colon in the notation of source—for example, the effects *(sp:s)* and *(psq:s)* in our example. These effects are confounded with the effects of the facets that remain in the notation after the letter that appears on both sides of the colon is deleted; that is, *(sq:s)* is confounded with *(q)*, and *(psq:s)* is confounded with *(pq)*. On this basis, one can identify the variance components that can be estimated as well as the effects that are confounded in estimation of each component. In the Pilliner example, five components can be estimated: *(p)*, *(s)*, *(q:s)*, *(ps)*, and *(pq:s)*. Two effects cannot be estimated: *(sq:s)*, because it is confounded with *(q:s)*, and *(psq:s)*, because it is confounded with *(pq:s)*.

Although identification of the confounded effects does not enter into the calculation procedures in phase one, it can be important for interpretation of the results of subsequent estimations. For example, when interpreting the contribution of the variance component *(q:s)* to overall error variance, it should be recognized that this component includes two potential sources of variation: Q and SQ.

Graphic Representation of the Observation Design. Using the diagrammatic conventions proposed by Cronbach and others (1972), we can represent an observation design with as many as four crossed facets and with any number of nested facets. Crossed facets are represented by ellipses that intersect; nested facets are represented by concentric ellipses. The observation design of Pilliner's study is depicted in Figure 2.

The diagram should include as many regions as there are variance components to be estimated. The regions that appear within a single ellipse correspond to the nonnested main effect components—for example, $\sigma^2(p)$ and $\sigma^2(s)$. Regions within several concentric ellipses represent nested main effect components—for example, $\sigma^2(q{:}s)$. Regions located in the intersection of several ellipses correspond to the components for interaction effects among two or more facets. For example, $\sigma^2(pq{:}s)$ is situated within the intersection of the ellipse P and the ellipse Q:S.

Calculation of Sums of Squares, Degrees of Freedom, and Mean Squares. The rules of thumb described by Millman and Glass (1967) are applied in phase one to determine the equations for the calculation of the sum of squares, the degrees of freedom, and the mean square for each source of variation in the design. Table 1 displayed the results of these calculations for Pilliner's study. Since these procedures are generally well known, we will not present the derivation of the formulas for our example in any detail. We will show, however, how the graphic representation of the observation design can be used to verify the formulas for the sums of squares obtained by the rules of Millman and Glass.

Graphic Verification of the Formulas for the Sums of Squares. The rules that we propose will be illustrated for the equation of the sum of squares for $Q{:}S$ in Pilliner's study. For this source of variation, the formula obtained by the rules of Millman and Glass includes two terms:

$$\frac{1}{n_p}\overset{q}{E}\,\overset{s}{E}\,(\overset{p}{E}X)^2 \;-\; \frac{1}{n_p n_q}\overset{s}{E}\,(\overset{p}{E}\,\overset{q}{E}X)^2$$

Rule 1: For each term, find the union of the ellipse or ellipses that correspond to the facet or facets of the summation outside parentheses. (Disregard the correction term for the effect of the grand mean, for which a region does not exist.) Do the same separately for the ellipse or ellipses of the summation within parentheses. Subtract from the first region its intersection with the second.

Rule 2: For combining terms, add the regions for each term obtained by rule 1 algebraically, respecting the signs in the sum of squares formula. Using Rule 2, one obtains the region of the diagram with the notation corresponding to the effect (α) under consideration. As Figure 3 shows, these rules allow graphic verification of the formula of the sum of squares for any source represented in the observation design.

Estimation Procedures for Phase Two. Phase two uses the appropriate

Figure 2.

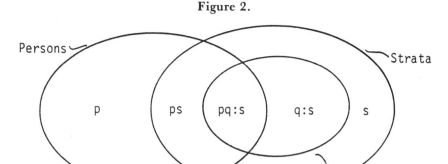

random or mixed model of analysis of variance, as determined by the mode of sampling of the levels of each facet to estimate the variance components. If a design includes finite or fixed facets, the usual statistical procedure is to formulate the equations for the expected mean squares directly in terms of the appropriate mixed model and to extract the variance component estimates from these equations. When conducting a generalizability analysis, it is more informative first to calculate the variance component estimates on the basis of the completely random model, then to recombine these estimates for the mixed model under consideration. This approach allows the estimates obtained under the two models to be compared. It can be carried out using general algorithms applicable to any type of design.

Random Model Estimates of Variance Components. The equation for estimating each variance component can be defined by the following general formula, developed from previous work by Tourneur (Tourneur and Cardinet, in press):

$$\hat{\sigma}^2(\alpha) = \frac{1}{f(\alpha)}\left[MS(\alpha) + \sum_{i=1}^{i=j}(-1)^i \left\{ \begin{array}{l} \text{sum of the mean squares whose} \\ \text{total subscripts contain } (\alpha), \\ \text{plus the letters for } i \text{ additional} \\ \text{facets, each of which appeared in} \\ \text{subscripts at step } (i-1) \text{ for } i>1 \end{array} \right\} \right]$$

where $f(\alpha)$ is the product of the numbers of observed levels of all facets that do not appear in the total subscript of the effect (α), j is the number of expressions entering into the summation, and i is the rank (from 1 to j) of the expression between parentheses. We will now apply this formula to estimate each variance component in the Pilliner example.

(1) $$\hat{\sigma}^2(pq{:}s) = MS\ (pq{:}s)$$

The variance component for the highest-order interaction is estimated by the corresponding mean square that includes the letters of all facets of the design in its subscript.

Figure 3. Graphic Verification of the Sum of Squares Formula for the Effect ($q{:}s$)

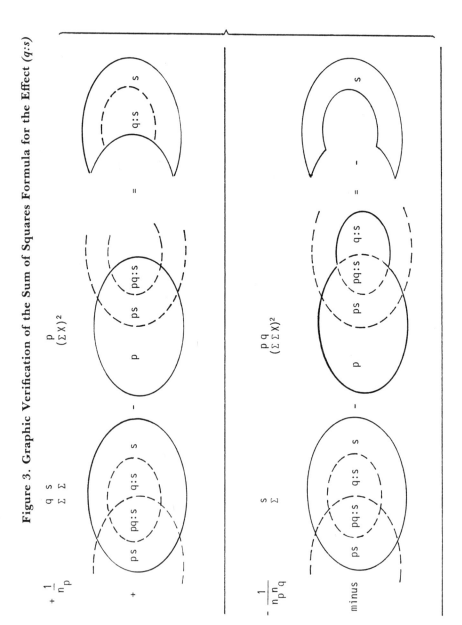

(2)
$$\hat{\sigma}^2(ps) = \frac{1}{n_q} \; [MS(ps) + (-1)^1 \; \{MS(pq{:}s)\}]$$

The coefficient is $\frac{1}{n_q}$ because the facet Q does not appear in the subscript (ps) of the effect under consideration. The mean square for $(pq{:}s)$ includes the effect (ps) plus one additional facet Q. This mean square appears between parentheses preceded by (-1) with an exponent of 1 because it is the first (and, in this case, the only) expression entering into the summation.

(3)
$$\hat{\sigma}^2(q{:}s) = \frac{1}{n_p} \; [MS(q{:}s) + (-1)^1 \; \{MS(pq{:}s)\}]$$

The explanations for the preceding component apply in this case as well.

(4)
$$\hat{\sigma}^2(s) = \frac{1}{n_p n_q} \; [MS(s) + (-1)^1 \; \{MS(ps) + MS(q{:}s)\} + (-1)^2 \{MS(pq{:}s)\}]$$

The coefficient is $\frac{1}{n_p n_q}$ because the facets P and Q do not appear in the subscript of the effect (s). Two mean squares, $MS(ps)$ and $MS(q{:}s)$, appear within the first set of parentheses because their subscripts contain (s) plus one and only one letter for another facet. This expression is preceded by (-1) with an exponent of 1 because it is the first step of the summation. At the second step of the summation, the exponent of (-1) changes to 2. The mean square for $(pq{:}s)$ appears in the second set of parentheses because its subscript contains (s) plus the letters of two other facets that appeared in the mean square subscripts within the first set of parentheses. If the letters p or q had not appeared in the previous expression of the summation, the term $MS(pq{:}s)$ would have been eliminated.

(5)
$$\hat{\sigma}^2(p) = \frac{1}{n_p n_q} \; [MS(p) + (-1)^1 \; \{MS(ps)\}]$$

$MS(ps)$ appears in the first set of parentheses because it contains (p) plus the letter for one and only one other facet. Although the mean square for $(pq{:}s)$ includes (p) plus the letters from two additional facets, the formula does not include a second expression of the form $(-1)^2 \{MS(pq{:}s)\}$ because the letter q does not appear in the subscript of the mean square within the first set of parentheses.

For designs that include fixed or finite facets, if one obtains a negative estimate of a variance component, one retains it, since it represents merely an intermediate step toward the estimation of the appropriate mixed model component.

Graphic Verification of the Random Model Formulas. The formulas for estimation of the random model variance components can be verified by the following rule:

Rule 3: Locate the region corresponding to the component (α) under consideration in the diagram of the observation design. Locate the ellipse or intersection of ellipses that corresponds to the mean square of the effect (α). Subtract from, or add to, the area just identified the ellipses or intersection of ellipses that corresponds to the other mean squares appearing in the formula of $\hat{\sigma}^2(\alpha)$. Control so that each region complementary to (α) is extracted once and only once from the area of $MS(\alpha)$. The expression obtained by rule 3 is preceded by the appropriate coefficient $\dfrac{1}{f(\alpha)}$. Figure 4 illustrates the application of this rule for the variance components of the Pilliner example.

Mixed Model Estimates of Variance Components. To obtain the mixed model estimate of a variance component (α), one adds to the random model estimate $\hat{\sigma}^2(\alpha)$ a weighted sum of the other random model components that contain (α) in their total subscripts. A general formula for mixed model estimates is described by Brennan (in press):

$$\hat{\sigma}^2(\alpha \,|\, \mathbf{M}) = \hat{\sigma}^2(\alpha) + \sum_j \frac{\hat{\sigma}^2(\beta_j)}{f(\beta_j)}$$

where $\hat{\sigma}^2(\alpha)$ is the random model estimate for the effect (α), $\hat{\sigma}^2(\alpha)(\alpha \,|\, \mathbf{M})$ is the corresponding mixed model estimate for (α), $\sigma^2(\beta_\sigma)$ is the random model estimate of all other components that include all letters of the component (α) in their total subscripts, and $f(\beta_j)$ is the product of the numbers of admissible levels of the facets appearing in the subscript of β_j but not in the subscript (α). If the subscript of a component includes the letters of purely random facets other than those of (α), the denominator $f(\beta_j)$ is infinity, and this term of the summation is eliminated. If the letters supplementary to (α) correspond to finite or fixed facets, a fraction of $\sigma^2(\beta_j)$ is added to $\sigma^2(\alpha)$. For fixed facets, this fraction is based on n_i or N_i (number of observed levels = number of admissible levels); for finite facets, the fraction is based on N_i (number of admissible levels $N_i > n_i$).

For the Pilliner example, let us suppose that the three strata are randomly sampled from five areas of arithmetic operations, while the other facets *(P and Q)* are sampled from infinite populations. Given this mixed model $\mathbf{M}_1$, the variance components are estimated as follows:

$$
\begin{aligned}
\hat{\sigma}^2(p \,|\, \mathbf{M}_1) &= \hat{\sigma}^2(p) + \hat{\sigma}^2(ps)/5 \\
\hat{\sigma}^2(s \,|\, \mathbf{M}_1) &= \hat{\sigma}^2(s) \\
\hat{\sigma}^2(q{:}s \,|\, \mathbf{M}_1) &= \hat{\sigma}^2(q{:}s) \\
\hat{\sigma}^2(ps \,|\, \mathbf{M}_1) &= \hat{\sigma}^2(ps) \\
\hat{\sigma}^2(pq{:}s \,|\, \mathbf{M}_1) &= \hat{\sigma}^2(pq{:}s)
\end{aligned}
$$

In this case, only the component for persons is modified.

Figure 4.

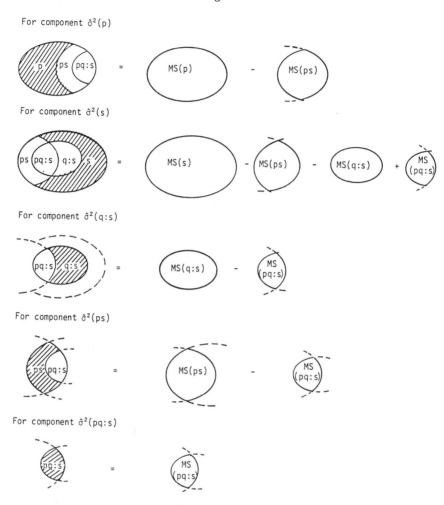

Let us now suppose that, in addition to purely random sampling of questions and finite random sampling of strata, the twenty-eight subjects constitute a fixed group of pupils taught by a particular teacher with a special method in a nonreplicable situation. In this case, the facet P would be fixed, and the components for a second mixed model $\mathbf{M_2}$ would be estimated as follows:

$$\hat{\sigma}^2(p\,|\,\mathbf{M_2}) = \hat{\sigma}^2(p) + \hat{\sigma}^2(ps)/5$$
$$\hat{\sigma}^2(s\,|\,\mathbf{M_2}) = \hat{\sigma}^2(s) + \hat{\sigma}^2(ps)/28$$
$$\hat{\sigma}^2(q{:}s\,|\,\mathbf{M_2}) = \hat{\sigma}^2(q{:}s) + \hat{\sigma}^2(pq{:}s)/28$$
$$\hat{\sigma}^2(ps\,|\,\mathbf{M_2}) = \hat{\sigma}^2(ps)$$
$$\hat{\sigma}^2(pq{:}s\,|\,\mathbf{M_2}) = \hat{\sigma}^2(pq{:}s)$$

Under this mixed model, the estimates of the variance components are modified for questions and for strata as well as for persons.

Graphic Verification of the Mixed Model Formulas. Having drawn a diagram of the estimation design as defined by rule 4 that follows, one can then identify the terms of the formula for each mixed model component as indicated in rule 5.

Rule 4: Draw the ellipses of fixed facets with dotted lines and the ellipses of finite random facets with dashed lines. Draw the purely random facets with solid lines.

Rule 5: To find the terms of the formula for the mixed model component $\hat{\sigma}^2(\alpha \mid M)$, add to the random model component for (α) the components of interaction with (α) that are adjacent to the region of (α), providing that they can be reached by crossing a dotted or dashed line.

Each component of interaction added to $\hat{\sigma}^2(\alpha)$ is divided by the appropriate coefficient $f(\beta_j)$. Figure 5 diagrams the estimation design for the mixed model M_2 just described. The arrows indicate the application of rule 5 for the verification of the mixed model estimation formulas.

Numerical Estimates from the Data of Pilliner's Study. Using the random model formulas, one obtains the following estimates of the variance components:

$$\hat{\sigma}^2(pq{:}s) = MS(pq{:}s) = 0.1572$$
$$\hat{\sigma}^2(ps) = (1/n_q)[MS(ps)MS(pq{:}s)] = (1/25) \cdot (0.2322 - 0.1572)$$
$$= 0.0030$$

**Figure 5. Estimation Design for Calculation of
Mixed Model Variance Components**

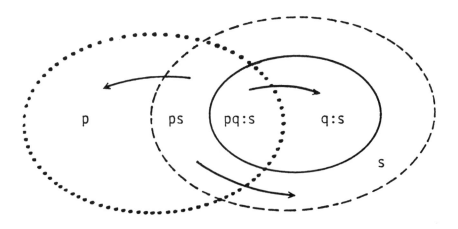

Note: . . . . represents fixed facets
------------------ represents facets involving finite sampling
————————— represents random facets

$$\hat{\sigma}^2(q{:}s) \quad = (1/n_p)[MS(q{:}d)] = (1/28)\cdot(1.3550 - 0.1572)$$
$$0.0428$$

$$\hat{\sigma}^2(s) \quad (1/(n_p n_q))[MS(s) - MS(ps) - MS(q{:}s) + MS(pq{:}s)]$$
$$= (1/(28\cdot25))[2.1066 - 0.2322 - 1.3550 + 0.1572]$$
$$= 0.0010$$

$$\hat{\sigma}^2(p) \quad = (1/n_s n_q)[MS(p) - MS(ps)] = (1/75)\cdot(3.7092 - 0.2322)$$
$$= 0.0463$$

The adjusted estimates for the mixed model M_2—with random sampling of three strata from a population of five and with the persons facet fixed—are calculated as follows:

$$\hat{\sigma}^2(pq{:}s\,|\,\mathbf{M}) = 0.1572$$

$$\hat{\sigma}^2(ps\,|\,\mathbf{M}) \quad = \hat{\sigma}^2(ps) = 0.0030$$

$$\hat{\sigma}^2(q{:}s\,|\,\mathbf{M}) \quad = \hat{\sigma}^2(q{:}s) + \hat{\sigma}^2(pq{:}s)/N_p$$
$$= 0.0428 + (1/28)(0.1572) = 0.0484$$

$$\hat{\sigma}^2(s\,|\,\mathbf{M}) \quad = \hat{\sigma}^2(s) + \hat{\sigma}^2(ps)/N_p$$
$$= 0.0010 + (1/28)(0.0030) = 0.0011$$

$$\hat{\sigma}^2(p\,|\,\mathbf{M}) \quad = \hat{\sigma}^2(p) + \hat{\sigma}^2(ps)/N_s$$
$$= 0.0463 + (1/5)(0.0030) = 0.0469$$

In this example, the estimates obtained with the random and mixed models are nearly the same due to the small magnitude of the interaction *PS* and to the relatively large number of levels of the facet *P*. In other cases, however, there may be substantial differences between the random model and the corresponding mixed model components.

Algorithms for Phase Three

The calculations used in phases one and two are based on general analysis of variance procedures that are not oriented toward any particular aim of measurement. Within the framework of analysis of variance, failure to answer a test question correctly on a given occasion is merely an observation coded as zero. To interpret this observation in the context of generalizability theory, one must specify the object of study. Depending on the purpose of measurement, the object of study can be the child (who has not learned something), the question (which does not reveal what the child knows), or the occasion (which does not allow the child to demonstrate his knowledge). The choice of a reference point is necessary for extraction of measurements from the observed data. To estimate generalizability parameters, facets of the design that correspond to the objects of measurement must be distinguished from facets of the design that correspond to the instruments of measurement.

The measurement design defined in phase three specified the allocation of facets with respect to the two faces of measurement: the face of differentiation (**D** face) and the face of instrumentation (**I** face). The number of possible measurement designs increases as the number of facets in the design increases. If all facets for the Pilliner example are formed by random sampling, the following measurement designs can be defined:

D face	I face	Object of Study
P, S	Q:S	results of persons with respect to each of the strata (assuming that $\sigma^2(q)$ is equal for each stratum)
P	Q:S, S	results of persons in the overall domain of arithmetic covered by the test
S	P, Q:S	difficulty levels of the strata
Q:S	P	difficulty levels of the questions within strata (eliminating the interstrata variation and assuming that $\sigma^2(q)$ is homogeneous across strata)
S, Q:S	P	difficulty levels of the questions pooled for all strata

Definition of the Measurement Design. To estimate generalizability parameters, it is necessary to consider both the mode of sampling of the levels of each facet (random, fixed) and the role of each facet in measurement (differentiation, instrumentation). The following notation can be used to designate the types of facets appearing in a measurement design:

$$M(D^R/D^F/I^F/I^R)$$

The letter **M** before the parenthesis indicates a measurement design defined in phase three. (The letter **O** will be used for optimization designs defined in phase four.) Inside parentheses, one or more facets appear between slashes according to the following conventions: differentiation facets (D^R) formed by random sampling are indicated in the first position, even if they are finite. Fixed differentiation facets (D^F) are noted in the second position. Fixed instrumentation (I^F), referred to here as *control facets*, appear in the third position. Instrumentation facets (I^R) formed by random sampling appear in the final position. These facets of generalization are essential to any generalizability study. They can be finite. A measurement design can include all four types of facets, but it must always include at least one type of differentiation facet (D^R or D^F) and at least one facet of generalization (D^R). If a certain type of facet is absent, a dash replaces its symbol in notation of the design.

Given the second mixed model estimation design defined previously for Pilliner's study, one can specify two measurement designs:

$$\mathbf{M}_1(-/P/-/S, Q:S)$$
$$\mathbf{M}_2(S/-/P/Q:S)$$

The first design $\mathbf{M}_1$ applies if the aim is to measure the abilities of persons belonging to a particular fixed group while generalizing with respect to all admissible questions and strata. The second design $\mathbf{M}_2$ applies if one wishes to compare the difficulty levels of randomly selected strata while generalizing over questions as answered by a fixed group of persons.

A graphic representation of a measurement design can be obtained from the diagram of the estimation design adopted in phase two by outlining the ellipses of the differentiation facets in red and the ellipses of the generalization facets in blue. The ellipses of the control facets are left uncolored. For the Pilliner example, in the diagram of the measurement design $\mathbf{M}_1$ $(-/P/-/S, Q:S)$, the ellipse of the facet P would be outlined in red, and the ellipses of the facets S and $Q:S$ would be outlined in blue. In the diagram of the design $\mathbf{M}_2$ $(S/-/P/Q:S)$, the ellipse of the facet S would appear in red, the ellipse of $Q:S$ would appear in blue, and the ellipse of the fixed instrumentation facet P would remain uncolored.

Control of Coherence. Many designs include one or more facets nested in other facets—for example, pupils nested in classes or in socioeconomic strata. If a nested facet is the object of study (that is, a $\mathbf{D}$ facet), the superordinate facet or facets in which it is nested must also belong to the $\mathbf{D}$ face of the design.

When one facet is nested in another facet, the interaction between them is confounded with the variance of the nested facet. Since the interaction of a $\mathbf{D}$ facet with a generalization facet is a component of error as defined by Cronbach and others (1972), the nesting of a $\mathbf{D}$ facet in an $\mathbf{I}^R$ facet implies a confounding of error variance with differentiation variance. In that case, a generalizability analysis can not be conducted. Thus, a $\mathbf{D}$ facet cannot be nested in a generalization facet. It is also necessary to exclude the nesting of a differentiation facet in a control ($\mathbf{I}^F$) facet. If each of the objects to be differentiated is observed under a single level of a superordinate facet, it is impossible to sum the effects of the levels of the $\mathbf{I}^F$ facet for each object. These principles imply that, for the Pilliner example, it would be incoherent to consider analysis of the designs $\mathbf{M}_3$ $(Q:S/-/P/S)$ and $\mathbf{M}_4$ $(Q:S/P/-/S)$.

It is simple to verify the coherence of a measurement design graphically. After outlining the differentiation facets in red, one checks to see that no red ellipses are nested in other kinds of ellipses.

Active and Passive Variance. Although fixed instrumentation facets affect estimation of the variance components in phase two, they do not enter into estimation of generalizability parameters in phase three. If all admissible levels of an instrumentation facet are present in the design, neither the main effects nor the interaction effects of the facet are a source of random sampling error affecting the reliability of measurement. Consequently, all components that include an $\mathbf{I^F}$ facet in their primary subscript can be disregarded in the subsequent steps of analysis. Since these components do not reflect random sampling fluctuations, they are termed *passive variance*, in contrast to the components of active variance entering into the estimation of generalizability parameters.

For our example of the measurement design $\mathbf{M_2}$, in which persons constitute a fixed instrumentation facet, there are three components of passive variance: $\hat{\sigma}^2(p\,|\,\mathbf{M})$, $\hat{\sigma}^2(ps\,|\,\mathbf{M})$, $\hat{\sigma}^2(pq{:}s\,|\,\mathbf{M})$ and only two components of active variance: $\hat{\sigma}^2(s\,|\,\mathbf{M})$, $\hat{\sigma}^2(q{:}s\,|\,\mathbf{M})$. This example shows how important it is to dissociate the procedures of analysis of variance from the procedures based on generalizability theory. Although the effects of the facet P are totally disregarded in phase three, estimation of the active variance components in phase two is affected by the fixed status of the facet P.

Since the $\mathbf{I^F}$ facets do not enter into subsequent calculations in phase three, they can be deleted from the diagram of the measurement design at this point. The letters designating such facets should, however, continue to appear in the subscripts of the other variance components. The coefficients used in the error formulas will be based on the number of levels of both the fixed and the random instrumentation facets.

Expectancies of Variance. The definitions of variance components used by Cornfield and Tukey (1956) coincide with those of Cronbach and others (1972). In particular, when the number of admissible levels of a facet is finite, Cronbach and others and Cornfield and Tukey use a definition of variance in which the denominator is $N - 1$ for primary indices and N for nesting indices.

For the Pilliner example, the mixed model components as defined by Cornfield and Tukey are (E designates expected value):

Component	Cornfield and Tukey (1956)
$\hat{\sigma}^2(p\,\|\,\mathbf{M})$	$\Sigma_p(\tilde{\mu}_p)^2/(N_p-1)$
$\hat{\sigma}^2(s\,\|\,\mathbf{M})$	$\Sigma_s(\tilde{\mu}_s)^2/(N_s-1)$
$\hat{\sigma}^2(q{:}s\,\|\,\mathbf{M})$	$\Sigma_s[E(\tilde{\mu}_{q:s})^2]N_s$
$\hat{\sigma}^2(ps\,\|\,\mathbf{M})$	$\Sigma_s\Sigma_p(\tilde{\mu}_{ps})^2/(N_p-1)(N_s-1)$
$\hat{\sigma}^2(pq{:}s\,\|\,\mathbf{M})$	$\Sigma_s\Sigma_p[E(\tilde{\mu}_{pq:s})^2]/(N_p-1)N_s$

where $\tilde{\mu}_\alpha$ is the score effect for the component α.

Although the procedures of analysis of variance that we use in phases one and two are based on the definitions of Cornfield and Tukey, for some purposes we find it necessary to introduce a correction in phase three in order to estimate certain generalizability parameters. This correction implies an adjustment of all variance component estimates that include a fixed or finite random facet in their primary subscripts. Each component is multiplied by $(N_f-1)/N_f$, where N_f is the number of admissible levels of the fixed or finite facet under consideration. This adjustment coefficient in applied for each fixed or finite facet included in the primary subscript of the estimated variiance component. For sake of clarity, the adjusted components are termed *expectancies of variance*; they are designated by $E^2(\alpha)$.

For the Pilliner example, the adjusted estimates of variance components are calculated as follows:

$$E^2(p) = [(N_p - 1)/N_p]\hat{\sigma}^2(p \mid M_2) = (27/28)(0.0469) = 0.0452$$

$$E^2(s) = [(N_s - 1)/N_s]\hat{\sigma}^2(s \mid M_2) = (4/5)(0.0011) = 0.0009$$

$$E^2(q{:}s) = \hat{\sigma}^2(q{:}s \mid M_2) = 0.0484$$

$$E^2(ps) = [(N_p - 1)(N_s - 1)/N_p N_s]\hat{\sigma}^2(ps \mid M_2) = [(27{-}4)/(28 \cdot 5)](0.0030)$$
$$= 0.0023$$

$$E^2(pq{:}s) = [(N_p - 1)/N_p]\hat{\sigma}^2(pq{:}s \mid M_2) = (27/28)(0.1572) = 0.1516$$

Once these adjustments have been made, we can proceed to estimate generalizability parameters for the measurement design under consideration.

Diagram of the Measurement Design. It is useful at this point to indicate on the diagram of the measurement design the three areas that will serve as graphic references for the estimation of the generalizability parameters. To identify these three areas, draw simple blue slashes (/////) over the entire area of the blue ellipses corresponding to the facets of generalization. Add red oblique slashes over the area of the intersection of the blue ellipses (generalization facets) with the red ellipses (differentiation facets). The area of the red ellipses that is specific to the differentiation facets remains without slashes. This area contains the variance components that enter into estimation of the variance of differentiation. The areas with slashes include the components that enter into the estimates of absolute and relative error variance. Figure 6 applies these conventions in black and white to the diagram of the design for $M_1(-/P/-/S, Q{:}S)$.

Differentiation Variance. The variance of differentiation is defined as the expected value of the variance of the universe scores of the objects of study. In most classical generalizability studies described by Cronbach and others (1972), the objects of study constitute a single facet. The estimated variance component for this facet is thus the only element that enters into estimation of the variance of differentiation.

When the **D** face of a measurement design is composed of several facets, the population to be differentiated is constituted by the Cartesian product of the levels of the crossed **D** facets plus the union of the levels of all nested **D** facets. The universe scores of the members of this population are determined by the main effects of the **D** facets and by the interactions among the **D** facets. Since the procedures of analysis of variance assure independent estimates of each effect, the variance of the universe scores is equal to the sum of the variances of the score components.

The variance of differentiation $\sigma^2(\tau)$ is estimated by the following general algorithm: Identify the components of active variance that include

Figure 6. Measurement Design M_1 $(-/P/-/S,\ Q{:}S)$

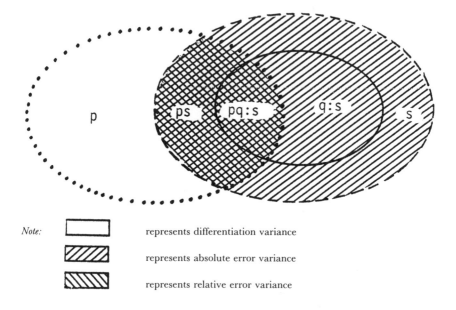

Note: ▭ represents differentiation variance

▨ represents absolute error variance

▨ represents relative error variance

only **D** facets in their primary subscripts, and add the (adjusted) estimates of these variance components.

Applying this rule to the measurement design M_1 $(-/P/-/S, Q{:}S)$, one obtains the following estimate of the differentiation variance:

$$\hat{\sigma}^2(\tau) = E^2(p) = 0.0452$$

For the design M_2 $(S/-/P/Q{:}S)$, the estimate is:

$$\hat{\sigma}^2(\tau) = E^2(s) = 0.0009$$

If one wished to differentiate the difficulty levels of all questions pooled across strata, the **D** face would be composed of two facets, $Q{:}S$ and S, and the variance of differentiation would be estimated as follows:

$$\hat{\sigma}^2(\tau) = E^2(s) + \hat{\sigma}^2(q{:}s\,|\,M) = 0.0009 + 0.0484 = 0.0493$$

Because questions are nested in strata, the interaction QS is confounded with the component for $Q{:}S$.

In a diagram of the measurement design, the components that enter into the estimate of the variance of differentiation are those that appear in the area without slashes; that is, in the area of the red ellipses that does not intersect with the blue ellipses. In the diagram of the design $\mathbf{M}_1$ shown in Figure 6, this area contains a single component for the main effect of the facet P.

Absolute and Relative Error. The terms *absolute error* and *relative error* are abbreviations of the expressions *random error of observation associated with absolute measurement* and *random error of observation associated with relative measurement.* Following Cronbach and others (1972), we use the symbol δ to designate error that affects the relative positions of the objects of study and that thereby reduces the precision of measurement for comparative decisions based on observed deviation scores. For comparisons of persons based on a crossed $p \times I$ design, relative error is defined as

$$\delta_{pI} = (\mathbf{X}_{pI} - \mu_I) - (\mu_p - \mu)$$

The variance of relative error is denoted by $\sigma^2(\delta)$. Absolute error (Δ) affects the precision of measurement in situations where observed scores are used as estimates of the universe scores of the objects of study. For the $p \times I$ design, absolute error is defined as

$$\Delta_{pI} = \mathbf{X}_{pI} - \mu_p.$$

It includes relative error as well as the systematic error that is specific to the instrument.

$$\delta_{pI} + (\mu_I - \mu) = (\mathbf{X}_{pI} - \mu_I) - (\mu_p - \mu) + (\mu_I - \mu)$$
$$= \mathbf{X}_{pI} - \mu_p = \Delta_{pI}$$

The variance of absolute error is symbolized by $\sigma^2(\Delta)$.

Estimation of Absolute Error Variance. The variance of absolute error is composed of all components of active variance that include at least one facet of generalization in their total subscript. It is estimated by a weighted sum of all (adjusted) variance component estimates that remain part of the active variance after extraction of the components that enter into the variance of differentiation.

Each variance component estimate is divided by the number of observed levels (n_i) of each facet of instrumentation that appears in its total subscript. This formula corresponds to the well-known formula for the standard error of the mean: When observations are drawn randomly from an infinite population, the error variance is inversely proportional to the size of the sample.

With finite random facets, the standard error formula is based not only on the sample size but also on its relationship to the size of the population sampled:

$$\sigma^2_{\overline{\mathbf{X}}} = \frac{\sigma^2}{n_i} \left(\frac{N_i - n_i}{N_i - 1} \right)$$

The only way in which this formula differs from the previous formula is that it introduces the multiplicative factor $(N - n)/(N - 1)$, called the *finite population correction*. This correction must be introduced for each random finite facet that appears in the primary subscript of a component.

It is obvious that the finite population correction equals one and that it is unnecessary when N_i tends to infinity, which is the case with purely random facets. Inversely, if a facet I is fixed in the primary subscript (that is, if $N_i = N_i$), the finite population correction becomes zero, and the variance component makes no contribution to error variance. This case has already been dealt with by eliminating the components of passive variance.

Thus, to estimate the absolute error variance, identify all components of active variance that remain after extraction of the components that enter into the variance of differentiation. Next, divide each (adjusted) variance component estimate by the product of the number of observed levels of the I facets in the total subscript of the component. For each random finite I facet that appears in the primary subscript of a component, multiply the term just obtained by the corresponding finite population correction $(N_i - n_i)/(N_i - 1)$. Finally, add these terms to obtain $\hat{\sigma}^2(\Delta)$.

For the measurement design $\mathbf{M}_1$ $(-/P/-/S, Q{:}S)$ of the Pilliner example, the estimate of absolute error variance includes all estimated variance components except $E^2(p)$. Four terms, corresponding to the sources S, $Q{:}S$, PS, and $PQ{:}S$, are added with the appropriate coefficients. The sources S and PS are divided by n_s; the sources $Q{:}S$ and $PQ{:}S$ are divided by $n_s \cdot n_q$.

The finite population correction is necessary for the terms $E^2(s)$ and $E^2(ps)$, but it does not apply to the terms $\sigma^2(p{:}s|M)$ and $E^2(pq{:}s)$. The limitation of sampling fluctuations on the facet S reduces the estimated error variance for the effects (s) and (ps). Since $\sigma^2(q{:}s)$ and $\sigma^2(pq{:}s)$ are assumed to be homogeneous for all strata, their contributions to estimated error variance are not affected by the size of the population from which the strata are sampled.

$$
\begin{aligned}
\hat{\sigma}^2(\Delta) = \quad & \left[\frac{E^2(s)}{n_s} \cdot \frac{N_s - n_s}{N_s - 1}\right] + \frac{\hat{\sigma}^2(q{:}s|M)}{n_s \cdot n_q} \\[2mm]
+ \, & \left[\frac{E^2(ps)}{n_s} \cdot \frac{N_s - n_s}{N_s - 1}\right] + \frac{E^2(pq{:}s)}{n_s \cdot n_q} \\[2mm]
= \quad & \left[\frac{0.0009}{3} \cdot \frac{5 - 3}{5 - 1}\right] + \frac{0.0484}{3 \cdot 25} \\[2mm]
+ \, & \left[\frac{0.0023}{3} \cdot \frac{5 - 3}{5 - 1}\right] + \frac{0.1516}{3 \cdot 25} \\[2mm]
= \quad & 0.0032
\end{aligned}
$$

For the measurement design $\mathbf{M}_2$ $(S/-/P/Q{:}S)$, the active variance includes only two components, $E^2(s)$ and $\hat{\sigma}^2(q{:}s|M)$. The absolute error variance is thus estimated by a single component:

$$\hat{\sigma}^2(\Delta) = \hat{\sigma}^2(q{:}s\,|\,\mu)/n_q = 0.0484/25 = 0.0019$$

One can refer to the diagram of the measurement design to verify that the equation for estimating the absolute error variance includes terms corresponding to all regions located inside the total area of the blue ellipses; that is, inside the area covered by simple slashes and by crossed slashes. This graphic verification is particularly useful for complex designs that involve a large number of facets.

Estimation of Relative Error Variance. As Cronbach and others define relative error variance, estimation of this parameter includes the components of interaction between the **D** facets crossed with the facets of generalization as well as the components of the facets of generalization that are nested in **D** facets. However, this intuitive definition can lead to errors when designs are complex. A more systematic procedure is to add, with their coefficients, all components of $\sigma^2(\Delta)$ that include at least one **D** facet in their total subscripts.

Applying this rule for the design M_1 of the Pilliner example, one obtains the following estimate of $\hat{\sigma}^2(\delta)$:

$$\hat{\sigma}^2(\delta) = [\{E^2(ps)\cdot(N_s - n_s)\}/\{n_s\cdot(N_s - 1)\}] + [E^2(ps{:}s)/(n_s\cdot n_q)]$$
$$= 0.0023/6 + 0.1516/(3\cdot25) = 0.0024$$

For the design M_2, the estimates of relative and absolute error variance are the same:

$$\hat{\sigma}^2(\delta) = \sigma^2(\Delta) = \hat{\sigma}^2(q{:}s\,|\,M)/25 = 0.0019$$

By referring to the diagram of the measurement design, one can verify that the equation for the estimation of relative error variance includes terms corresponding to all regions inside the intersection of the red and the blue ellipses; that is, to the regions covered by crossed slashes.

Margins of Error. The estimates of absolute error variance and relative error variance can be used to determine confidence intervals that indicate the magnitude of the random sampling fluctuations that affect the measurements obtained with a given design. A confidence interval can be established around a selected value C that is of interest for theoretical or practical reasons; for example, to define a proportion of correct answers as a cutoff score required to pass an examination composed of questions drawn at random. In this case, the formula $C \pm Z_{\alpha/2}\hat{\sigma}(\Delta)$ is used for a $(1 - \alpha)$ percent confidence interval based on the appropriate value from the standard normal (Z) distribution and the square root of the estimate of absolute error variance. It is also possible to define a cutoff score on the scale of the deviation scores; for example, as one standard deviation above the mean of the observed sample: $C = \bar{X} + \hat{\sigma}$. The confidence interval can then be computed by the formula $C \pm Z_{\alpha/2}\hat{\sigma}(\delta)$. The confidence interval is based on the estimate of relative error, because use of deviation scores eliminates the random fluctuations affecting the mean value for each condition of measurement.

We will use the term *margin of error* to denote confidence intervals established for the difference between any two measurements obtained with a given design. Depending on the type of comparison that is of interest—absolute or relative—the formula for the margin of error includes the corresponding estimate of error variance:

$$\pm Z_{\alpha/2} \sqrt{2\hat{\sigma}^2(\Delta \text{ or } \delta)}$$

This interval indicates the degree of difference between two measurements that can be attributed, with a probability of $(1 - \alpha)$ percent, to random sampling fluctuations in the conditions of measurement.

To make relative comparisons of students' performance on the arithmetic test in Pilliner's study, one can calculate the following margin of error, using $Z = 1.96$ for a 95 percent confidence interval:

$$\pm 1.96 \sqrt{2(0.0024)} = 0.1358$$

This value pertains to a difference expressed in terms of an average score per item; that is, to the total test score divided by the number of test items. For a test of seventy-five items, a difference between two scores would have to be larger than $(0.1358) \times (75)$—that is, larger than 11—in order to be interpreted as reflecting a true difference in the relative levels of students' competence; that is, in the universe deviation scores.

Coefficients of Generalizability. A generalizability coefficient is an overall indicator of the degree of precision provided by a measurement design, given the type of differentiation and the sources of sampling error specified in the design. It is defined as a ratio $\hat{E}\varrho^2$, with the expected value of the variance of differentiation in the numerator and the expected value of the variance of the observed scores in the denominator. The second value is equal to the variance of differentiation $\sigma^2(\tau)$ plus the error variance, $\sigma^2(\Delta)$ or $\sigma^2(\delta)$, that is appropriate for the type of measurement (absolute or relative) to be undertaken. Generalizability coefficients are calculated on the basis of the estimated differentiation and error variances by the following formulas:

$$\hat{E}\varrho^2(\Delta) = \frac{\hat{\sigma}^2(\tau)}{\hat{\sigma}^2(\tau) + \hat{\sigma}^2(\Delta)}$$

$$\hat{E}\varrho^2(\delta) = \frac{\hat{\sigma}^2(\tau)}{\hat{\sigma}^2(\tau) + \hat{\sigma}^2(\delta)}$$

For absolute and relative differentiation of persons based on design $\mathbf{M}_1$ in the Pilliner example, the following coefficients can be calculated:

$$\hat{E}\varrho^2(\Delta) = \frac{0.0452}{0.0452 + 0.0032} = 0.934$$

$$\hat{E}\varrho^2(\delta) = \frac{0.0452}{0.0452 + 0.0024} = 0.950$$

For the differentiation of strata in the design $\mathbf{M}_2$, $\hat{\sigma}^2(\Delta) = \hat{\sigma}^2(\delta)$; thus, only a single coefficient can be calculated.

$$\hat{E}\varrho^2(\Delta) = \frac{0.0009}{0.0009 + 0.0019} = 0.321$$

This coefficient shows that Pilliner's design would be inadequate for comparisons of achievement levels attained for different strata of arithmetic items. In contrast, the generalizability coefficients for the design $\mathbf{M}_1$ indicate a very high degree of reliability for the differentiation of pupil achievement levels. It is possible, moreover, for a shortened version of the test to be used without appreciable loss of reliability. This consideration is addressed in phase four.

Procedures for Phase Four

A major interest of generalizability analysis is the use of information obtained in phases one, two, and three to determine ways of improving the design for subsequent research or decision making. The improvements introduced in phase four can have several aims: improving precision by reducing measurement error, eliminating sources of bias introduced by certain facets of the **D** face, or reducing data collection costs while maintaining an acceptable level of reliability. This optimization phase does not entail the application of any specific algorithms. Rather, for each type of modification that is considered, the appropriate algorithms of the preceding phases are reapplied to new combinations of existing data. We will indicate briefly the types of modifications that can be introduced for the designs defined in each of the preceding phases. A detailed discussion of these modifications is presented by Cardinet and others (1981, 1982).

The most fundamental modifications concern the structure of the observation design itself. For example, one can consider changing a crossed facet into a nested facet. Estimates of generalizability parameters for the new design can then be obtained by recombining the estimated variance components calculated for the existing design.

The estimation design can be modified by considering possible changes in the mode of sampling of the levels of facets, provided that such changes can be justified on logical and practical grounds. For example, a random generalization facet can be changed into a fixed or a finite random instrumentation facet. In this case, appropriate mixed model estimates of variance components are calculated, and the estimates of the generalizability parameters are modified accordingly. This type of modification reduces the random sampling fluctuations that contribute to measurement error, but it also restricts the generality of interpretation of the resulting measures. Modifications of the mode of sampling of **D** facets can also be considered, but the net effect is difficult to predict, since the estimates of both the differentiation and the error variances are affected.

Modifications of the measurement design entail changes in the allocation of the facets with respect to the **D** and **I** faces. One can decide, for example, to transfer a facet of differentiation to the face of instrumentation. In this case, the scores of the objects remaining on the **D** face have to be calculated as an average over the levels of the new **I** facet. To eliminate measurement bias due to the effects of a superordinate **D** facet (such as sex or socioeconomic stauts), one can decide to establish separate designs for each level of the nesting facet. Generalizability parameters have then to be estimated separately for each subpopulation.

One of the modifications most often encountered increases the number of observed levels along one or more **I** facets of the design in order to control the principal sources of random sampling error. This modification generally implies increasing the sample of observed levels for the facets that make large contributions to the components of error variance while (if it is necessary to maintain costs at a constant level) reducing the number of levels for facets that make weak contributions to error. It is also possible to consider decreasing sample size so as to reduce costs while maintaining a given level of reliability. For the measurement design $\mathbf{M_1}$ of the Pilliner example, one can maintain reliability at 0.80 for the differentiation of persons while making a substantial reduction in the initial sample of twenty-five items per stratum. For absolute measurement, a sample of six items per stratum is sufficient:

$$\hat{\sigma}^2(\Delta) = 0.0116, \qquad \hat{E}\varrho^2 = 0.80$$

For relative measurement, a sample of only five items per stratum is needed:

$$\hat{\sigma}^2(\delta) = 0.0105, \qquad \hat{E}\varrho^2 = 0.81$$

If an observation design is to be used for several different measurement purposes, it may be necessary to consider trade-offs between the directions of optimization that are desirable for each object of study.

Presentation of a Complex Example

The algorithms proposed for phases one, two, and three can easily be applied to designs of much greater complexity than those typically dealt with in publications on generalizability theory. We will illustrate the ease of application with the observation, estimation, and measurement designs used for a survey of mathematics achievement by Tourneur and Cardinet (1981).

The observation design included six facets: D (content domains of mathematics, crossed with the five other facets), F (test forms, in which two facets — series and classes — are nested), $S:F$ (parallel series of test questions composed of one question per domain and nested in test forms), $C:F$ (classes nested in test forms but crossed with series of questions — each class received three series of questions nested in a same test form), A (age groups in which pupils are nested, crossed with the other facets), and $P:AC:F$ (pupils crossed with series, nested in ages and in classes, with classes nested in forms). Because there is one question per domain in each series, the facet questions are confounded with the interaction between domains and series.

In the estimation design, forms, series, and classes were considered as purely random facets; pupils were considered as a finite random facet (four subjects having been selected in each class); and domains and ages were treated as fixed facets. The diagram of the estimation design is shown in Figure 7.

Given the multiple purposes of the survey, various measurement designs were defined and analyzed in order to determine the adequacy of data collection procedures for differentiations along each facet of the design. Figure 8 depicts the measurement design defined to differentiate achievement levels for fixed domains while generalizing over pupils, classes, forms, and series, with age as a fixed control facet: $M(-/D/A/P:AC:F, C:F, S:F, F)$.

Despite the complexity of the relationships among facets and the diversity of sampling modes, the formulas for the estimation of generalizability parameters can easily be defined by inspection of the diagram of the measurement design. Areas of the diagram covered by crossed slashes identify the components that enter into the estimate of relative error variance: DF, $DS:F$, $DC:F$, $SDC:F$, $DP:AC:F$, and $DSP:AC:F$. The estimate of absolute error variance includes all these components plus those in the area covered by simple slashes: F, $C:F$, $S:F$, $SC:F$, $SP:AC:F$, and $P:AC:F$. A single component D is used to estimate the differentiation variance. After identifying the components of each parameter, it is easy to write the estimation formulas using the algorithms proposed for phase three.

Advantages of the Proposed Framework

To conclude, we will summarize the major theoretical and practical advantages of the procedures and algorithms proposed in this chapter.

Clarification of Underlying Models. By clearly distinguishing the first two phases leading to the estimation of the variance components from the latter two phases centered on problems of measurements, the framework makes it possible to clarify the respective contributions of analysis of variance on the one hand and of generalizability theory on the other. In phase two, estimates of variance components are obtained by a general set of algorithms that take into account the mode of sampling of the levels of the facets, independent of any assumption about the object of measurement. After specifying the measurement design in phase three, one can pass from one model to the other by

Figure 7. Diagram of the Estimation Design for the Study by Tourneur and Cardinet (1981)

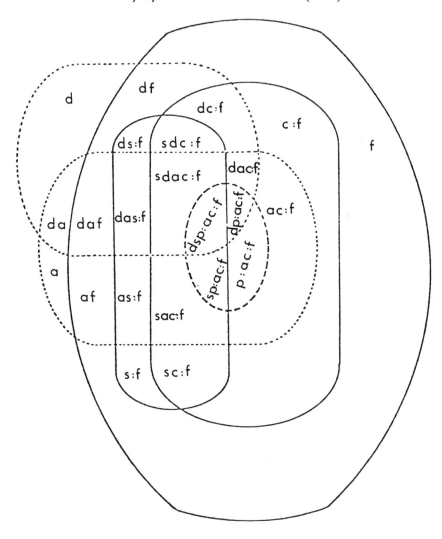

Note: .... represents purely fandom sampling of facets
--------------- represents finite random sampling of facets
———————— represents fixed sampling of facets

Figure 8. Diagram of the Measurement Design
M(− /D/A/P:AC:F, C:F, S:F, F)

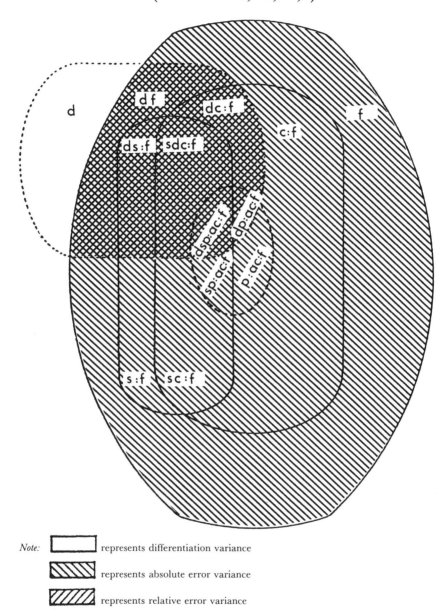

Note: ▢ represents differentiation variance

▨ represents absolute error variance

▨ represents relative error variance

applying a simple adjustment algorithm. This approach permits a simplification of the formulas used for estimating generalizability parameters. After the components of passive variance are eliminated, a standard set of rules is applied to determine weighted sums of appropriate random or mixed model estimates of variance components.

Explication of the Two Faces of Measurement. In most existing presentations of generalizability theory and its applications, the conditions of measurement are defined explicitly by a series of facets, whereas the objects of study (generally persons) are treated implicitly. This approach fails to recognize that a generalizability coefficient has meaning only with respect to a well-defined population. In our framework, the definition of a measurement design implies specification not only of the universe of generalization (facets of the **D** face) but also of the population of differentiation (facets of the **D** face). This dual specification is necessary both for the interpretation of estimates of generalizability parameters and for the formulation of appropriate optimization designs.

Specification of the face of differentiation helps to clarify the purpose of measurement, particularly in cases where individual differences are not the object of measurement. For example, in situations of mastery learning, where all pupils are expected to attain the instructional objectives at the end of the course of study, the classical perspective of interindividual differentiation does not apply. Criterion-referenced measurement designs can, however, be developed in order to carry out differentiation along other facets, such as groups of persons (masters versus nonmasters), stages of learning (beginning versus end of the course of study), categories of objectives (comprehension versus application), and learning strategies (students classified according to behavioral indicators). By clearly specifying the facets of the **D** face, the principles of generalizability theory can be used to improve the construction of procedures appropriate to the type of differentiation that is sought.

Parallel Analysis of the Two Faces of Measurement. Since allocation of the facets of a design to the two faces of measurement is not inherent in the data, any type of facet (persons, items, occasions) can be allocated either to the face of differentiation or to the face of instrumentation, depending on the aim of measurement. The operations defined in classical presentations of generalizability theory for analysis of the faces of instrumentation can therefore be transposed to analysis of the face of differentiation. The variance of differentiation can be estimated by the sum of the independent effects of several **D** facets and their interactions. Once the sources of differentiation variance have been estimated, they can be judged as acceptable or unacceptable, valid or invalid with respect to the aim of measurement. Techniques for the redefinition of facets analogous to item analysis can thus be applied with respect to both faces of the design in order to improve the generalizability of the measures. Analysis of the contributions of the components of differentiation variance is particularly useful for identifying bias due to the effects of superordinate nesting facets; for example, to effects of socioeconomic status when differentiating persons and to effects of form of presentation when differentiating achievement levels for instructional objectives. By parallel analysis of the two faces of the design, optimization can take two directions: increasing precision by reducing error or eliminating bias by modifying the design or making statistical adjustments (for example, by using deviation scores).

Analysis of Mixed Model Designs. In contrast to existing presentations of generalizability theory, which assume at least implicitly that the objects of study are randomly sampled from an infinite population, our framework allows for treatment of fixed and finite random facets on the face of differentiation. Our framework is thus applicable to a wide range of situations, including educational surveys designed to differentiate achievement levels for a finite random sample of instructional objectives and classical experimental situations designed to differentiate the effects of two or more fixed treatments. The calculation of margins of error provides a useful reference point for various users of survey data. For experimental designs that involve a large number of sources of random sampling fluctuations, our framework makes margins of error easier to calculate than the statistical F test does.

Analysis of Complex Designs. For mixed model designs that involve a large number of facets, the usual procedures of generalizability analysis entail extremely complicated equations for the estimation of generalizability parameters. In our framework, once the appropriate mixed model variance components have been estimated in phase two, a simple, standard set of rules can be applied to estimate generalizability parameters in phases three and four, however complex the measurement design may be. The only limit on application of the procedures that we propose lies in the increasing instability of the estimates of variance components as the number of sources of variation increases.

The use of diagrams at each stage of analysis provides a concrete graphic representation of the design under consideration as well as a means of verifying the estimation formulas. The diagram of the measurement design is particularly useful in identifying the variance components that enter into the equations for estimating each generalizability parameter. It can also help to define valid F tests for complex experimental designs.

In summary, then, the procedures proposed in this chapter can be considered as taking a step in the direction blazed by Cronbach and his collaborators (1963, 1972). In contrast to such pioneers of psychometrics as Spearman, Thurstone, and Gulliksen, who developed measurement concepts and procedures in a relatively isolated manner, the formulation of generalizability theory represents a major effort to integrate the problems of measurement with the broad field of general statistics. Although our proposals emphasize certain distinctions between generalizability theory and analysis of variance, they also enlarge the conception of generalizability as a theory of statistical measurement applicable not only to persons but to any object of study in the social sciences.

48

References

Brennan, R. L. *Elements of Generalizability Theory.* Iowa City: American College Testing Program, 1983.

Brennan, R., Jarjoura, D., and Deaton, E. *Some Issues Concerning the Estimation and Interpretation of Variance Components in Generalizability Theory.* ACT Technical Bulletin no. 36. Iowa City: American College Testing Program, 1980.

Cardinet, J., Tourneur, Y, and Allal, L. "Extension of Generalizability Theory and Its Applications in Educational Measurement." *Journal of Educational Measurement,* 1981, *18,* 183–204; and 1982, *19,* 331–332.

Cornfield, J., and Tukey, J. "Average Values of Mean Squares in Factorials." *Annals of Mathematical Statistics,* 1956, *27,* 907–949.

Cronbach, L., Rajaratnam, N., and Gleser, G. "Theory of Generalizability: A Liberalization of Reliability Theory." *British Journal of Mathematical and Statistical Psychology,* 1963, *16,* 137–163.

Cronbach, L., Gleser, G., Nanda, H., and Rajaratnam, N. *The Dependability of Behavioral Measurements: Theory of Generalizability for Scores and Profiles.* New York: Wiley, 1972.

Millman, J., and Glass, G. V. "Rules of Thumb for the ANOVA Table." *Journal of Educational Measurement,* 1967, *4,* 41–51.

Pilliner, A. E. G. "The Application of Analysis of Variance Components in Psychometric Experimentation." Unpublished doctoral dissertation, University of Edinburgh, 1965.

Tourneur, Y., and Cardinet, J. "L'étude de généralisabilité d'un survey [The Study of Survey Generalizability)." *Education et Recherche,* 1981, *3,* 33–50.

Tourneur, Y., and Cardinet, J. *De l'observation à la mesure: Théorie de la généralisabilité [From Observation to Measurement: Theory of Generalizability.]* Bern: Peter Lang, in press.

Jean Cardinet is a professor at the Institute Romand de Recherches et de Documentation Pedagogiques, Neuchatel, Switzerland.

Linda Allal is a professor at the University of Geneva, Geneva, Switzerland.

The external validity of research findings can be defined in terms of multilevel and cross-level inference from a generalizability perspective.

Multilevel Analysis and Cross-Level Inference of Validity Using Generalizability Theory

Leslie J. Fyans, Jr.

A major concern in the study of psychological and educational processes is the validity of theories and findings drawn from one setting, population, or culture for another setting, population, or culture. Should inferences concerning human behavior and contexts be general, lawful, and monothetic, or should they be particularized, specific, and unique? Operationally, this concern has been labeled the need for external validity (Campbell and Stanley, 1964), ecological inference (Langbein and Lichtman, 1978), or multilevel analysis (Przeworski and Teune, 1970). The argument is that a researcher must establish the generalizability of findings with unilevel designs. Unfortunately, the processes and factors that psychologists and educators study are multilevel in nature. All manner of effects or constraints are raised by variables at any number of levels such as home and family, classroom, school, district, state, and nation.

Conventional methods for establishing cross-level inference and generalizability of findings use multiple regression techniques (Burstein, 1976, 1978; Burstein and others, 1978). However, Burstein (1980) describes nine difficulties raised by use of the regression model approach to conduct multilevel studies and derive cross-level inferences. These difficulties involve con-

L. J. Fyans, Jr. (Ed.). *Generalizability Theory: Inferences and Practical Applications.*
New Directions for Testing and Measurement, no. 18. San Francisco: Jossey-Bass, June 1983.

sistency, specification bias, efficiency of estimation, generality to make complex models, variable efficiency, collinearity effects, aggregation gain, and preconditions necessary for assessing group differences. However, when the processes of generalizability theory are coupled with Bayesian methodology, they provide a unified system for determining the validity of findings across multiple levels of inquiry and for using empirically defined validity to define regression equations that predict cross-level effects. Moreover, techniques for comparing contemporary results computationally with baseline, normative, or longitudinal trends can be adduced as well as techniques for comparing growth or change among individuals, as in the case of criterion-referenced, mastery, and tailored testing. Finally, extensions can be made to render scales or items metrically equivalent.

All these Bayesian generalizability techniques are computationally tractable; essentially, they are based on manipulation of variance components drawn from standard analysis of variance and covariance. A number of authors have used these methods with real life educational and psychological constructs and data (Fyans and Maehr, 1979, 1982; Fyans and others, 1981, 1983; Salili and others, 1981; Sprague and others, 1981).

In this chapter, I will illustrate the Bayesian generalizability approach just described by a hypothetical multilevel cross-cultural study on attributional behavior in several different national groups. For the purposes of illustration, culture will be the highest level in the design; any other facet, such as region, (as with N.A.E.P. comparisons) or state, or school district, could have been used instead.

Theoretical Framework and Model

The researcher in our hypothetical cross-cultural study on attributional behavior is a social psychologist. He is interested in the attributional behavior of students in situations where they experience success relative to their performance on a task. The researcher wants to know whether success attributions can be accounted for solely in terms of individual differences in achievement motivation, or whether they depend on the individual's ethnic or cultural characteristics. He also wants to know whether differences in success attributions depend on differences in age or developmental level and whether cultural, ethnic, or age differences impose limitations.

The analysis of variance model implied by this researcher's concerns is that of a partially hierarchical design (Winer, 1971) with two nested factors, age and achievement motivation level. If C represents the cultural facet; E, ethnicity; T, levels of achievement motivation; and A, age level, this design, in the notation proposed by Cronbach and others (1972) is $(E:C) X A X T$. We will assume that the analysis of variance model follows a random effects model based on the postulate of exchangeability (Novick and Jackson, 1974; Winkler, 1972; Turner, 1967; Kaplan, 1964). We will also assume that the prior density functions for each facet in the study do not express perturbations around any specific point (Box and Tiao, 1973; Zellner, 1971).

Sequential Decision Strategy

For our hypothetical example, assessment of the veridical level of generality (or specificity) consists of four steps; each step investigates the generalizability coefficient for a different level in the study. For our example, these four steps correspond roughly to the levels of individual actor, subculture, and culture suggested by Przeworski and Teune (1970). The decision process begins with computation of the variance components for each term produced by the analysis of variance. Next, each of these components is transformed into a generalizability coefficient, using any interactions that the independent variable of interest has with any other variable as an error term $\sigma^2(\delta)$. In terms of our hypothetical analysis of variance, the following generalizability coefficients can be derived:

$$\varrho^2 \text{ (culture)} = \frac{\sigma^2 \text{ (culture)}}{\text{(culture)} + \sigma^2(\delta)}$$

where $\sigma^2(\delta) = \sigma^2$ (culture × age) + (culture × achievement motivation level) + σ^2 (culture × age × achievement motivation level) + σ^2 (within cell).

$$\varrho^2 \text{ (ethnic group)} = \frac{\sigma^2 \text{ (ethnic group)}}{\sigma^2 \text{ (ethnic group)} + \sigma^2(\delta)}$$

where $\sigma^2(\delta) = \sigma^2$ (ethnic groups × age level) + σ^2 (ethnic groups × achievement motivation levels) + σ^2 (ethnic groups × age level × achievement motivation level) + σ^2 (within cell).

$$\varrho^2 \text{ (age level)} = \frac{\sigma^2 \text{ (age level)}}{\varrho^2 \text{ (age level)} + \sigma^2(\delta)}$$

where $\sigma^2(\delta) = \sigma^2$ (age level × culture) + σ^2 (age level × ethnic groups) + (age level × achievement motivation level) + σ^2 (age level × culture × achievement motivation level) + σ^2 (age level × ethnic groups × achievement motivation level) + σ^2 (within cell).

$$\varrho^2 \text{ (achievement motivation level)} = \frac{\text{(achievement motivation level)}}{\sigma^2 \text{ (achievement motivation level)} + \sigma^2(\delta)}$$

where $\sigma^2(\delta) = \sigma^2$ (achievement motivation level × culture) + σ^2(achievement motivation level × ethnic groups) + σ^2 (achievement motivation level × age level) + σ^2 (achievement motivation level × culture × age level) + σ^2 (achievement motivation level × ethnic group × age level) + σ^2 (within cell).

Before I describe the sequential decision strategy with which these generalizability coefficients are manipulated, it seems worthwhile to discuss the meaning of the size of generalizability coefficients. A large generalizability coefficient for a particular independent variable represents a high within-level correlation among the achievement motivation scores for that independent variable. Thus, a high generalizability coefficient for the independent variable age would mean that, within each age level (for example, high school, college), achievement motivation scores were highly similar but that they displayed large differences across age levels. Thus, all discussions or statements concerning achievement behavior would have to be made specific to an individual's age level. Thus, the high generalizability coefficient would indicate a high degree of generalizability of achievement motivation behavior across all other nonage factors in the study (such as sex, cultural membership, ethnic group membership, achievement motivation level, and so forth). In the same way, a high generalizability coefficient for culture would indicate a high within-culture correlation among achievement motivation scores, and it would imply that there was a high degree of generalizability of achievement scores across the other nonculture facets in the study (such as age, sex, achievement motivation level, ethnic group membership, and so forth). Thus, a high generalizability coefficient for culture would imply that all statements concerning achievement scores would have to be made specific to each individual culture.

A low generalizability coefficient for a particular independent variable indicates that achievement motivation scores have little or no specificity for the independent variable of interest, because a low generalizability coefficient indicates that the independent variable of interest accounts for little or no achievement score variance. Thus, a low generalizability coefficient can mean that any within-level dependent variable relationship has been attentuated by interaction with other terms.

After computing these coefficients, the research sequentially determines which level accounts for the most variance in the dependent variable. The researcher's determination is based on the magnitude of the generalizability coefficient for each level in the study. If the researcher begins at what Przeworski and Teune (1970) call the level of the individual actor, the researcher examines the magnitude of ϱ^2 (achievement motivation) to decide whether the success attribution scores can be explained solely in terms of individual differences—this makes them generalizable across age groups, ethnic groups, and cultures—or whether the explanation has to be more specific and relative. If the ϱ^2 (achievement motivation) indicates that individual subjects do not form a single homogeneous population (Rohner, 1975; Malewski, 1961), the researcher continues on to the next level: that of age group differences (the subcultural level, in the terminology of Przeworski and Teune, 1970).

In checking the ϱ^2 (age groups), the researcher wants to determine whether there was generality across cultures and ethnic groups or whether the explanation of success attributions has to be specific to each developmental level. If a large amount of dependent variable variance is accounted for by ϱ^2 (ethnic groups), explanation of success attributions can be generalized across persons in different developmental levels, but it is specific to ethnic groups within each culture. If ϱ^2 (ethnic groups) is small, the researcher moves to the level of culture. If ϱ^2 (culture) is large, the researcher can conclude that characteristics unique to each culture (Triandis, 1972, 1975) account for the variance of success attributions.

However, it is possible for the interaction terms, not the main effects, to account for the plurality of the variance in dependent variables. Indeed, in both education and psychology, the interaction terms are often the most representative model of reality (Fyans, 1979). For example, Bowers (1973) describes several instances in research on strong person × situation interaction components. Cronbach and Snow (1977) discuss the interaction between certain aptitudes and instructional methods. Multilevel research by Fyans and Maehr (1982) uncovered interaction terms, such as culture × sex × age, sex × academic self-concept, and sex × home self-concept, that accounted for a substantial portion of achievement variance. Fyans and others (1981) found similar strong interaction effects for sex × grade × evaluation condition. Unfortunately, existing models of multilevel and cross-level analysis (Burstein, 1980) cannot deal with these all too prevalent interaction effects. Previous multilevel analytic approach would have to use response surface (Myers, 1976) approach to evaluate these multilevel or cross-level interaction effects. However, using the generalizability approach described here in line with suggestions by Golding (1975), one can obtain a generalizability coefficient for each interaction term in the model. To compute this coefficient, one places the variance component for the interaction term of interest in the numerator. In the denominator, one places the variance component for that interaction term plus the variance component for any other interaction term that contributes to the expected mean square of the interaction component of interest.

The interpretation of large generalizability coefficients for interaction terms is relatively straightforward. Essentially, the presence of a strong interaction effect means that the effects of that interaction term are externally valid across other components of the model that are not involved in the interaction term of interest. Thus, if there is a strong interaction effect for sex × achievement motivation level in our hypothetical example, that interaction effect can be said to be generalizable across the other non–sex × achievement motivation level components. That is, the interaction effect of sex × achievement motivation level is generalizable over cultures and age levels included in the study. The reader is encouraged to review the discussions of generalizability coefficients for interaction terms provided by Fyans and Maehr (1979, 1982), by Fyans (1979) and by Salili, Maehr, and Fyans (1981).

Data collected and analyzed for Sprague and others (1981) illustrate how this generalizability strategy can be used in multilevel research. The study of Sprague and others used data from teacher ratings of hyperactive behavior among approximately 9,000 students in West Germany, prerevolutionary Iran, New Zealand, the United States, and Venezuela. Analysis revealed five teacher rating factors that could be analyzed cross-culturally: fidgeting and restlessness (factor 1); defiance and stubbornness (factor 2); submissiveness (factor 3); attention deficit (factor 4); and social unacceptance (factor 5). Table 1 displays the generalizability multilevel for factor 1 ratings. The levels in this analysis include culture, student sex, and student age, which was nested in culture. The multilevel results for factor 1 indicate little if any specificity of differences due to cultural differences. Next, two differences are seen at the subcultural level: There are age differences, and there is a sex-by-age interaction effect. Thus, age differences are generalizable across cultures. Finally, at an even more specific level, there are differences in the ratings of fidgeting and restlessness in terms of sex-by-age interaction. That interaction effect is generalizable across all five cultures studied. Thus, statements and conclusions about fidgeting and restlessness can be made across cultures but focused on specific sex-by-age interaction profiles.

Estimation of Universe Scores in Multilevel and Cross-Level Studies

After determining the level of generalizability, the researcher may wish to use that generalizability information to predict the dependent variable. Cronbach and others (1972) discuss four linear regression formulas based on the level of generalizability. Those formulas are a version of Kelley's (1927, 1947) weighted average estimation. The revision by Cronbach and others of the Kelley prediction equation can be recast in a Bayesian manner for estimation in multilevel designs (Lindley, 1976; Novick, 1969). The resulting Bayesian equation surmounts the weaknesses of the equation on which it is based (Jackson, 1972; Novick and Jackson, 1970, 1974; Davis, 1975; Novick and others, 1971; Hill, 1970; Zellner, 1971; Box and Tiao, 1973; Jeffreys, 1961). The advantages of the Bayesian universe score equation over the

Table 1. Cross-Cultural Generalizability Analysis of
Fidgeting and Restlessness (Factor 1)

Level	Variance Component	Generalizability Coefficient
Culture	1.38	.004
Sex	1.74	.005
Age	46.88	.14
Culture × Age	0.04	.000
Sex × Age	292.50	.850
Culture × Sex × Age	0.00	.000
Error	2.30	.007

results obtained with existing observed score approaches (Burstein, 1980) and the classic Cronbach-Kelley approach can be summarized as follows: First, the Bayesian regression equation based on generalizability theory incorporates all available worthwhile and relevant information in its predictions. As Novick (1969) and Lindley (1976) have emphasized, for any one individual's observed score, there is collateral information about that individual's score from all the other individuals included in the study. Thus, once we have collected information on several individuals, we have some information about the scores of a newly measured individual. The regression model proposed here can use all this information in its predictions. Specifically, the information incorporated in the regression equation springs from three sources: The individual's score, the scores or performance of the group of which the individual is a member (within-group information) and information about members of other groups included in the study (between-group information). The conventional multi-level framework (Przeworski and Teune, 1970; Burstein, 1980) does not incorporate information from all three sources. Novick and Jackson (1970) see the use of all three kinds of information as critical to accurate predictions.

Second, in line with the reasoning just stated, research shows that this Bayesian full-information regression approach increases the precision of prediction. Cronbach and others (1972) illustrate the increased precision of prediction that results from incorporation of both within-group and between-group information in the same estimation equation. Similarly, Novick and Thayer (1969), Novick and others (1971), and Jackson and others (1971) have shown that adopting the collateral information Bayesian approach increases accuracy. Shigemasu (1976) and Novick and others (1972) point to a decrease in the mean square error of prediction when they use the Bayesian regression model.

Third, the Bayesian regression equation directly incorporates information regarding the level of generalizability found in the multilevel study. This incorporation is accomplished by use of the generalizability coefficient for the level of interest in the design. Increasing the number of levels of interest simply increases the number of distinct generalizability coefficient terms in the equation. Thus, only one basic regression equation is necessary. It is modified by the generalizability coefficient that is employed, which is based on the levels of interest for prediction. The regression model based on generalizability should be compared to the complex situation of contemporary multilevel analysis (Burstein, 1980; Przeworksi and Teune, 1970).

The generalizability coefficient employed in the equation can be composed of meaningful interactions among the independent variables. While these interactions tend to reflect a particularizing effect in terms of the generalizability issue, the representation of their effects can be theoretically very meaningful and important. The strength of these theoretically interesting interactions is explicitly expressed in the predicted scores via their inclusion in the definition of the generalizability coefficient.

Fourth, the confidence intervals that the researcher is able to make for the scores predicted by the equations are tighter than those for the scores predicted by conventional means. The scores predicted by the generalizability equations are based on a scale with a standard deviation defined by $\sigma\{\epsilon\}$. The observed scores predicted by the conventional models (Burstein, 1980) are based on a scale with a standard deviation of $\sigma\{\Delta\}$. Cronbach and others (1972) show that $\sigma\{\Delta\}$ is always greater than $\sigma\{\epsilon\}$. Thus, the researcher can use the same level of confidence for the universe scores that he uses with observed scores, but the interval is much shorter.

Fifth, a major advantage of this generalizability model concerns the use of prior information for any particular level in the design. This advantage is becoming increasingly important, especially for longitudinal data, for normative comparisons, in sequential testing of mastery or competency learning, in assessing intrastudent growth, and for base rate information. Thus, in estimating a student's universe score, the researcher can incorporate prior or collateral information. For example, in estimating a student's universe score, the normative performance of students in similar characteristics can be used as collateral information. In a mastery learning or tailored testing situation, information about the student's previous performance can be used as previous information and the student's contemporary performance can be used as the likelihood function to generate the universe score estimate.

Use of this Bayesian generalizability approach to estimate universe scores can be illustrated by the following example: A district superintendent conducts an analysis to determine both the average level of performance in mathematics of the seniors in each high school in the district and the district average. The district superintendent wishes to use this institutional research to estimate the scores of individual senior students in each school. Thus, the district superintendent is in essence conducting a cross-level inferential study; that is, he is using findings collected at the level of the district and the school to understand the performance of individual students. To obtain the students' level estimates, the superintendent can use the following Bayesian generalizability formula:

$$(1) \qquad\qquad Y = X \ldots + \varrho^2(Xp. - X..)$$

where Y is an individual student's predicted universe score on the mathematics test, ϱ^2 is the generalizability coefficient for students' mathematics performance across the district, $X \ldots$ is the grand mean across all high schools in the district, $X..$ is the mean of the school that the individual student attends, and Xp is the individual senior student's mathematics score.

This model uses all the information that the superintendent has concerning the mathematics performance of seniors to estimate the performance of individual students. Thus, the context in which the individual student performs — school as well as district — is called upon to enhance the prediction.

The standard error to be used with the estimated universe score above can be obtained by the formula:

(2)
$$\sigma\{\epsilon\} = \sigma\{p\}\{1 - \varrho\}$$

where $\sigma\{p\}$ is the variance component for students calculated by the superintendent and ϱ is the generalizability coefficient for the performance of senior students.

The district superintendent can feel confident that the estimated universe scores have less error than the raw observed scores, since the estimated scores reflect the reliability and external validity information concerning the mathematics results of students in his district. This confidence can be helpful when these estimated scores are used in decision circumstances, such as graduation, that require significant levels of confidence and credibility.

The general formula for this Bayesian regression is this:

(3)
$$Y = X\ldots + \varrho^2(Xp. - X..)$$

where Y is the estimated universe score; ϱ^2 is the generalizability coefficient for a given level of interest in the design, such as sex, $X\ldots$ is the grand mean of the dependent variable in the multilevel design; $X..$ is the mean of the subgroup on the dependent variable to which an individual belongs relevant to the level of interest, such as male or female; and Xp is an individual's score or performance on the dependent variable.

The determination of the level of interest can be based on theoretical reasoning or on the largest generalizability coefficient in the design. If more than one level is of theoretical interest or if the generalizability coefficient for more than one main effect or interaction term is relatively large, the equation can be expanded to incorporate the other levels, effects, and terms. The expansion occurs by adding terms such as the second term in equation 1 for each level wished. Here is an example that includes these levels:

(4)
$$Y = X\ldots + \varrho_1^2(Xp. - X^1.) + \varrho_2^2(Xp. - X^2.) + \varrho_3^2(Xp. - X^3.)$$

where $X\ldots$ is the grand mean across all students, $X^1., X^2., X^3.$, are the means for each level in the design (such as ethnic groups, grades, schools), $\varrho_1^2, \varrho_2^2, \varrho_3^2$ are the generalizability coefficients associated with each level in the design, and $Xp.$ is the individual student's score on the dependent variable.

Equation 1 can be decomposed into the variance components themselves:

(5)
$$Y = \frac{\sigma^2(Xp) + \sigma^2(\delta)(X..)}{\sigma^2 + \sigma^2(\delta)}$$

where σ^2 is the variance component for the level of interest, $\sigma^2(\delta)$ is the error or constraining variance components, and $Xp.$ and $X..$ are defined as for equation 1. This decomposition produces an added benefit, because it allows us to reduce the error in estimation variance even further. That is, Novick and Jackson (1974) have taken issue with the use of sample values for error variance and argued for regressed estimates of error variance. Using their developments and taking the value of $\sigma^2(\delta)$ from equation 5, we can obtain a regressed estimate of $\sigma^2(\delta)$ and then place the regressed value in equation 5.

Statistical Comparisons Based on Level of Generalizability

Information about the generalizability of a result transforms our knowledge of that result and our perspective on any subsequent analysis of the same result. That is, to use the term of Box and Tiao (1973) and Novick and Jackson (1974), we now have collateral information about the result that can change our inferences on the findings. Any future statistical tests become posterior inferences to the knowledge of the generalizability of the findings. Thus, obtaining information about the correlation of students' mathematics performance across several high schools — that is, about the generalizability of their mathematics performances — changes our capability for testing significant mean differences in students' mathematics performance across those schools. The generalizability information allows us to weight the statistical comparison and use knowledge that we have already obtained to reduce error in estimating significant differences.

Several traditional T and F tests between means can be presented that incorporate the generalizability information in the formula. These tests can be called *posterior significant tests*, since they are posterior to our obtaining knowledge of the level of generalizability. To illustrate, I will use language aimed at testing significant differences in achievement performance between schools. Obviously, we could use the same formula to compare statistically school district with statewide average performance.

Testing the Significant Difference Between Two Means. Let us use as an example the difference between two schools. The essential aim is to obtain estimates of the difference in light of the generalizability information. To obtain these estimates, we multiply the mean difference by the relevant generalizability coefficient:

$$\hat{d} = (\varrho^2)(\overline{X}_1 - \overline{X}_2)$$

The error term used to establish the credibility for this estimated difference is:

$$\sigma = \sqrt{2 \left[\frac{S_1 + S_2\,(1 - \varrho^2)}{JK - 1} \right] \left(\frac{\varrho^2}{K} \right)}$$

where S_1 is the within-school sum of squares, S_2 is the between-school sum of squares, J is the number of schools, and K is the number of observations within schools. The posterior credibility interval for testing the significance of this difference is:

$$\hat{d} \pm (\sigma)\,(t_{JK-1,\,1-\alpha})$$

Testing the Significance of the Difference Between Many Different Means and a Grand Mean. Let us use as an example the different means of individual schools and a grand mean such as that of a district or state. The formula for two mean differences can be extended to many different means as follows:

$$\phi = (M)(\varrho^2)$$

where M is the between-schools mean square, and ϱ^2 is the generalizability coefficient. The error term to test this comparison is:

$$\sigma = \frac{S_1 + (1-\varrho)S_2}{JK - 1}$$

where S_1 is the within-schools sum of squares, S_2 is the between-schools sum of squares, J is the number of schools, and K is the number of observations per school. The posterior credibility interval for this comparison is:

$$\Phi \pm (\sigma)(F_{J-1,\,JK-1,\,1-\alpha})$$

Estimates of Variance, Covariance, and Correlation in Light of Generalizability Information. Information about the generalizability of findings can influence one's beliefs posterior to obtaining the generalizability information about the values for the variance, covariance, and correlation in a set of student, school, or district means. Formulas for these calculations follow: The posterior variance for a school mean can be estimated by:

$$\mathrm{Var}\,(\Theta_j | \underset{\sim}{y}) = \frac{J(\nu_1 M_1 + \mu_1' \nu_2 M_2) - (J-1)\,(\mu_1' \nu_1 M_1 + \mu_2' \nu_2 M_2)}{JK(\nu_1 + \nu_2 - 2)} + (y_j. - y..)^2 \mu_2$$

where M_1 is the mean square within schools, M_2 is mean square between schools, J is the number of schools, K is the number of observations per school, $\underset{\sim}{y}$ is the vector of raw data,

$$\mu_1' \text{ is } \frac{(J-1)}{(J(K-1)2)}$$

$$\mu_2' \text{ is } \frac{(J+1)(J-1)}{(J(K-1)-4)(J(k-1)-2)}$$

μ_2 is $\mu_2' - (\mu_1')$, ν_1 is degrees of freedom for M_1, ν_2 is degrees of freedom for M_2, y_j is each school's mean on the dependent variable, and y.. is the grand mean on the dependent variable across all schools. The posterior covariance between the means of two schools can be estimated as follows:

$$\text{Cov }(\theta_i, \theta_j | \underset{\sim}{y}) = \frac{\upsilon_1\nu_1 M_1 + \mu_1\nu_2 M_2}{JK(\nu_1 + \nu_2 - 2)} + (y_i. - y..)(y_j. - y..)\mu_2$$

The posterior correlation between the means of two schools can be estimated as follows:

$$R(\theta_i, \theta_j | \underset{\sim}{y}) = \left[\frac{\text{Cov }(\theta_i, \theta_j | \underset{\sim}{y})}{\text{Var }(\theta_i | \underset{\sim}{y})\ \text{Var }(\theta_j | \underset{\sim}{y})} \right]^{1/2}$$

Posterior Density Function for ϱ^2

After computing the generalizability coefficients for each level in the study, the researcher is concerned about their reasonableness given the data at hand. To assess their reasonableness, the researcher can form the posterior density for each ϱ^2.

The posterior modes of the posterior distributions for the variance components and generalizability statistics of interest are both quite easy to obtain. The calculation of the modal (most likely) values of the posterior distribution is based on the definition of a χ^{-2} variate as $\chi^{-2}(X, \lambda, \nu)$, where X is the factor or component of interest, λ is the scale value for a particular χ^{-2}, and ν is degrees of freedom for a particular χ^{-2} distribution. The χ^{-2} distribution has the general form

$$\chi^{-2}(X, \lambda, \nu) = (K)\ (X)^{-\frac{1}{2}(\nu + 2)}\ e^{-\frac{1}{2}\left(\frac{\lambda}{X}\right)}$$

where K is a constant term. The modal (most likely) value of a distribution can be calculated by $\tilde{X} = \frac{\lambda}{\upsilon + 2}$ (Novick and Jackson, 1974).

Following this definition and discussion of the χ^{-2} distribution, the joint posterior density for composite factors of the hypothetical model presented earlier can be shown to take the form

$$p(V_T,\ V_{TC},\ V_{Te:c},\ V_e,\ V_{e:c},\ V_{i:e:c} | \underset{\sim}{y})$$

$$\chi^{-2}(V_T, SS_T, df_T) \cdot \chi^{-2}(V_{TC}, SS_{TC}, df_{TC}) \cdot \cdot \cdot \cdot \cdot$$

$$\cdot \cdot \cdot \cdot \chi^{-2}(V_{I:e:c}, SS_{I:e:c}, df_{I:e:c})$$

Thus, the joint mode $(\tilde{V})$ for the posterior distributions for any composite factor in the design can be obtained by dividing the sum of squares by the appropriate degrees of freedom plus two. The posterior modes for the partially hierarchical design of our hypothetical example are as follows:

$$\tilde{V}_T = \frac{SS_T}{df_T + 2}$$

$$\tilde{V}_C = \frac{SS_c}{df_C + 2}$$

$$\tilde{V}_{e:C} = \frac{SS_{e:c}}{df_{e:c} + 2}$$

$$\tilde{V}_{TC} = \frac{SS_{TC}}{df_{TC} + 2}$$

$$\tilde{V}_{Te:C} = \frac{SS_{Te:C}}{df_{Te:C} + 2}$$

$$\tilde{V}_{i:e:C} = \frac{SS_{i:e:C}}{df_{i:e:c} + 2}$$

(In this design, $SS_{i:e:c}$ is confounded with SS_{ϵ}, $\tilde{V}_{i:e:c}$ is confounded with $\tilde{V}_{\epsilon}$, and so on.)

This posterior modal framework can be extended to any partially hierarchical cross-level design. It will hold up as long as the posterior modal values satisfy the order established by the constraints of the model. However, if the constraint order is violated $\frac{SS_T}{df_T + 2} < \frac{SS_{TC}}{df_{TC} + 2}$, the Bayesian approach sets all composites involved equal to each other and uses a pooled estimate for the common value. Thus, if the order of the hypothetical posterior modal values of $\tilde{V}_T < \tilde{V}_{TC}$ was violated, then the Baysian rule would set $\tilde{V}_T = \tilde{V}_{TC}$ and estimate this common value by pooling

$$\frac{SS_T + SS_{TC}}{df_T + df_{TC} + 4}$$

After defining the posterior modal values for the composite factors in the design and taking care of any constraint conflicts, the researcher can estimate the posterior modal (most likely) values for the variance components in the partially hierarchical design. Estimates of the modes of the posterior distribution of variance components are derived from the estimates of the posterior modes of the composite factors of the partially hierarchical design. To estimate the posterior modes of the variance components that make up the composite factors, the researcher takes linear combinations of the composites. Thus, the posterior modal values for the variance components in the study of our example can be estimated as follows:

$$\tilde{\sigma}^2{}_T \quad = \frac{\tilde{V}_T - \tilde{V}_{TC}}{(i) \cdot (e) \cdot (c)}$$

$$\tilde{\sigma}^2{}_C \quad = \frac{\tilde{V}_C - \tilde{V}_{E:C} + \tilde{V}_{TC} - \tilde{V}_{TE:C}}{(i) \cdot (e) \cdot (t)}$$

$$\tilde{\sigma}^2{}_{E:c} \quad = \frac{\tilde{V}_{E:C} - \tilde{V}_{TE:C}}{(i) \cdot (t)}$$

$$\tilde{\sigma}^2{}_{TC} \quad = \frac{\tilde{V}_{TC} - \tilde{V}_{TE:C}}{(i) \cdot (c)}$$

$$\tilde{\sigma}^2{}_{Te:c} \quad = \frac{\tilde{V}_{TE:C} - \tilde{V}_{I:E:C}}{(i)}$$

$$\tilde{\sigma}^2{}_{I:E:C} = \frac{\tilde{V}_{I:E:C}}{(t)}$$

The solution to any ordering and constraint violation of the composite factors implies that the variance components for the composite factor that violates the order is estimated as equal to zero. Thus, if $\frac{SS_T}{df_T + 2} < \frac{SS_{TC}}{df_{TC} + 2}$, as it is in the preceding example, $\tilde{V}_T = \tilde{V}_{TC}$ and $\sigma^2{}_T = \frac{\tilde{V}_T - \tilde{V}_{TC}}{(i) \cdot (e) \cdot (c)} = 0$.

After calculating the posterior modes for the variance components in the design, the researcher can manipulate them according to the rules of generalizability theory to form the approximate posterior modal estimates for the appropriate generalizability statistics and coefficients. This manipulation follows the addition and division rules for the generalizability statistics for sample data alone. Thus, the model for $\tilde{\sigma}^2_T$ can be estimated by

$$\tilde{\sigma}^2(\delta) = \tilde{\sigma}^2{}_{TC/(c)} + \tilde{\sigma}^2{}_{TE:C/(e)(c)} + \tilde{\sigma}^2{}_{I:E:C/(i) \cdot (e) \cdot (c)}$$

the mode for $\tilde{\sigma}^2_C$ can be estimated by

$$\tilde{\sigma}^2(\delta) = \tilde{\sigma}^2{}_{TC/(t)} + \tilde{\sigma}^2{}_{TE:C/(t)(e)} + \tilde{\sigma}^2{}_{E:C/(e)} + \tilde{\sigma}^2{}_{I:E:C/(i) \cdot (e)}$$

and the mode for $\tilde{\sigma}^2_{E:C}$ can be estimated by

$$\tilde{\sigma}^2(\delta) = \tilde{\sigma}^2{}_{TE:C/(t) \cdot (c)} + \tilde{\sigma}^2{}_{I:E:C/(i) \cdot (c)}$$

These estimates of the modes of the posterior distributions of the $\tilde{\sigma}^2(\delta)$ statistics can then be used to estimate the posterior modes (most likely values) for the generalizability coefficients for the variables included in the design. The modes of the posterior distributions for the generalizability coefficient for the hypothetical study can be expressed as follows:

$$\tilde{\varrho}^2_{(T)} = \frac{\tilde{\sigma}^2_T}{\tilde{\sigma}^2_T + \sigma^2_{(\delta)T}}$$

$$\tilde{\varrho}^2_{(C)} = \frac{\tilde{\sigma}^2_c}{\tilde{\sigma}^2_c + \tilde{\sigma}^2_{(\delta)_c}}$$

$$\varrho^2_{(E:)C} = \frac{\tilde{\sigma}^2_{(E:C)}}{\tilde{\sigma}^2_{E:C} + \tilde{\sigma}^2_{(\delta)E:C}}$$

The sequential strategy described earlier in this chapter can then use these posterior modal estimates of the generalizability coefficients as statistics in making decisions. These posterior modal estimates of the generalizability coefficients have two advantages: They are the most likely values given the data at hand, and they can never assume a negative value.

Conclusion

This chapter presents several facets of a new approach that uses generalizability theory to conduct cross-level inference in psychological and educational research. Unlike past models for cross-level research, the new approach facilitates multiple-level investigations to test the external validity of results and findings. Based on generalizability analysis, the new model generates sequential tests of alternative hypotheses so that the veridical level of generality (or specificity) of the findings can succinctly be assessed. After determining the veridical level of generality empirically, the researcher can use a regression equation that incorporates all relevant information to construct cross-level predictions. Through use of Bayesian techniques and inference, this approach produces posterior distributions for the variance components and generalizability statistics that enable the researcher to evaluate their reasonableness. The Bayesian approach also incorporates information concerning the level of generalizability in tests between any means on the dependent variable. For all these reasons, the approach described here should aid researchers in the multilevel analysis and cross-level inference of validity in education and psychology.

References

Bendix, R. "Concepts and Generalization in Comparative Sociological Studies." *American Sociological Review,* 1963, *28,* 532–535.

Berry, J. W. "Introduction to Methodology." In H. C. Priandis, J. W. Berry (Eds.). *Handbook of Cross Cultural Psychology.* Vol. 2. Boston: Allyn and Bacon, 1980.

Bowers, K. S. "Situationism in Psychology: An Analysis and a Critique." *Psychological Review*, 1973, *80*, 307–336.

Box, G. E., and Tiao, G. C. *Bayesian Inference in Statistical Analysis*. Reading, Mass.: Addison-Wesley, 1973.

Brislin, R. W., Lonner, W. J., and Torndike, R. M. *Cross-Cultural Research Methods*. New York: Wiley, 1973.

Burstein, L. "The Choice of Unit of Analysis in the Investigation of School Effects: IEA in New Zealand." *New Zealand Journal of Educational Studies*, 1976, *11*, 11–24.

Burstein, L. "Alternative Approaches for Assessing Differences Between Groups and Individual-Level Coefficients." *Sociological Methodology and Research*, 1978, *7* (1), 5–28.

Burstein, L. "The Role of Level of Analysis in the Specificiation of Education Effects." In R. Dreeben and J. A. Thomas (Eds.), *The Analysis of Educational Productivity*. Cambridge, Mass.: Ballinger, 1980.

Burstein, L., Linn, R. L., and Capell, F. "Analyzing Multilevel Data in the Presence of Heterogenous Within-Class Regressions." *Journal of Educational Statistics*, 1978, *3*, 347–383.

Buss, A. R. "An Extension of Developmental Models that Separate Ontogenetic Changes and Cohort Differences." *Psychological Bulletin*, 1973, *80*, 466–479.

Buss, A. R. "More on the Age × Cohort Developmental Model: A Reply to La Bouvie." *Psychological Bulletin*, 1975, *82*, 170–173.

Campbell, D. T. "Natural Selection as an Epistemological Model." In R. Narroll and R. Cohen (Eds.), *A Handbook of Method in Cultural Anthropology*. New York: Columbia University Press, 1973.

Campbell, D. T., and Stanley, J. L. "Experimental and Quasi-Experimental Designs for Research on Teaching." In N. L. Gage (Ed.), *Handbook of Research on Teaching*. Chicago: Rand McNally, 1963.

Cohen, R. "Generalizations in Ethnology." In R. Narroll and R. Cohen (Eds.), *A Handbook of Method in Cultural Anthropology*. New York: Columbia University Press, 1973.

Cole, M., and Scribner, S. *Culture and Thought: A Psychological Introduction*. New York: Wiley, 1974.

Conger, A. J., and Lipshitz, R. "Measures of Reliability for Profiles and Test Batteries." *Psychometrika*, 1973, *38*, 411–427.

Cornfield, J., and Tukey, J. W. "Average Values of Mean Square Values in Factorials." *Annals of Mathematical Statistics*, 1956, *27*, 907–949.

Cronbach, L. J., Gleser, G. C., Nanda, H., and Rajaratnam, N. *The Dependability of Behavioral Measurements: Theory of Generalizability for Scores and Profiles*. New York: Wiley, 1972.

Cronbach, L. J., and Snow, R. E. *Aptitudes and Instructional Methods: A Handbook for Research on Interactions*. New York: Wiley, 1977.

Davis, C. *Bayesian Inference in Two-Way Analysis of Variance Models: An Approach to Generalizability*. Unpublished doctoral dissertation, University of Iowa, 1975.

Eckensbarger, L. H. "Methodological Issues of Cross-Cultural Research in Developmental Psychology." In J. R. Nesslroade and H. W. Reese (Eds.), *Life Span Developmental Psychology: Methodological Issues*. New York: Academic Press, 1973.

Fyans, L. J., Jr. "A New Multilevel Analytic Framework for Conducting Cross-Cultural and Socio-Cultural Psychological Research." *The Quarterly Newsletter of the Laboratory of Comparative Human Cognition*, 1979, *191* (3), 47–51.

Fyans, L. J., Jr., and Maehr, M. L. "Attributional Style, Task Selection, and Achievement." *Journal of Educational Psychology*, 1979, *71* (4), 499–507.

Fyans, L. J., Jr., and Maehr, M. L. "A Comparison of Sex Differences in Career and Achievement Motivation in Iran and the United States." *International Journal of Intercultural Relations*, 1982, *6*, 355–367.

Fyans, L. J., Jr., Maehr, M. L., Salili, F., and Desai, K. A. "A Cross-Cultural Exploration into the Meaning of Achievement." *Journal of Personality and Social Psychology,* 1983, *44* (5), 1000–1013.

Fyans, L. J., Jr., Kremer, B., Salili, F., and Maehr, M. L. "The Effects of Evaluation Conditions on Continuing Motivation: Study of Cultural, Personological, and Situational Antecedents of a Motivational Pattern." *International Journal of Intercultural Relations,* 1981, *5,* 1–22.

Golding, S. "Flies in the Ointment: Methodological Problems in the Analysis of the Percentage of Variance Due to Persons and Situations." *Psychological Bulletin,* 1975, *82,* 278–288.

Haller, A. O., Lewis, D. I., and Ishino, I. "The Hypothesis of Intersocietal Similarity in Occupational Prestige." *American Journal of Scoiology,* 1966, *71,* 115–127.

Hill, B. M. "Some Contrasts Between Bayesian and Classical Inferences in Analysis of Variance and Testing of Models." In L. Meyers and R. O. Collier, Jr. (Eds.), *Bayesian Statistics.* Itasca, Ill.: Peacock, 1970.

Irvine, S. H. "Tests as Inadvertant Sources of Discrimination in Personnel Decisions." In P. Watson (Ed.), *Psychology and Race.* London: Penguin Books, 1973.

Irvine, S. H., and Sanders, J. T. "Logic, Language, and Method in Construct Identification Across Cultures." In L. J. Cronbach and P. J. D. Drenth (Eds.), *Mental Tests and Cultural Anthropology.* The Hague: Mouton, 1972.

Jackson, P. H. "Simple Approximations in the Estimations of Many Parameters." *British Journal of Mathematical and Statistical Psychology,* 1972, *25,* 213–228.

Jackson, P. H., Novick, M. R., and Thayer, D. T. "Estimating Regressions in Groups." *British Journal of Mathematical and Statistical Psychology,* 1971, *24,* 129–153.

Jeffreys, H. *Theory of Probability.* Oxford, England: Clarendon, 1961.

Joe, G. W., and Woodward, J. A. "Some Developments in Multivariate Generalizability." *Psychometrika,* 1976, *41,* 205–217.

Kaplan, A. *The Conduct of Inquiry: Methodology for Behavioral Science.* Scranton, Pa.: Chandler, 1964.

Kelley, T. L. *Statistical Methods.* New York: Macmillan, 1927.

Kelley, T. L. *Fundamentals of Statistics.* Cambridge, Mass.: Harvard University Press, 1947.

LaBouvie, E. W. "An Extension of Developmental Models: Reply to Buss." *Psychological Bulletin,* 1975, *82,* 165–169.

Langbein, L. R., and Lichtman, A. J. *Ecological Inference.* Beverly Hills, Calif.: Sage, 1978.

Lindley, D. V. "The Estimation of Many Parameters." In V. P. Godambe and D. A. Sprott (Eds.), *Foundations of Statistical Inference.* Toronto: Holt, Rinehart and Winston, 1976.

McClelland, D. C. *The Achieving Society.* New York: Free Press, 1961.

Malewski, A. "Two Models of Sociology." *Studia Socjologiczne,* 1961, *1,* 341–349.

Miller, D. R. "The Personality as a System." In R. Naroll and R. Cohen (Eds.), *A Handbook of Method in Cultural Anthropology.* New York: Columbia University Press, 1973.

Murdock, G. P., and others. *Outline of Cultural Materials.* New Haven, Conn.: HRAF Press, 1967.

Naroll, R., and Cohen, R. (Eds.). *A Handbook of Method in Cultural Anthropology.* New York: Columbia University Press, 1973.

Novick, M. R. "Multiparameter Bayesian Indifference Procedures." *Journal of the Royal Statistical Society,* 1969, *31,* 29–64.

Novick, M. R., and Jackson, P. H. "Bayesian Guidance Technology." *Review of Educational Research,* 1970, *40,* 459–494.

Novick, M. R., and Jackson, P. H. *Statistical Methods for Educational and Psychological Research.* New York: McGraw-Hill, 1974.

66

Novick, M. R., Jackson, P. H., and Thayer, D. T. "Bayesian Inference and the Classical Test Theory Model: Reliability and True Scores." *Psychometrika,* 1971, *36,* 261–288.

Novick, M. R., Jackson, P. H., Thayer, D. T., and Cole, N. S. "Estimating Multiple Regression in M Groups: A Cross-Validation Study." *British Journal of Mathematical and Statistical Psychology,* 1972, *25,* 33–50.

Novick, M. R., and Thayer, D. T. *A Comparison of Bayesian Estimates of True Score* (ETS RB 69–74). Princeton, N.J.: Educational Testing Service, 1969.

Przeworski, A., and Tuene, H. *The Logic of Comparative Social Inquiry.* New York: Wiley, 1970.

Rohner, R. P. "Parental Acceptance–Rejection and Personality Development: A Universalist Approach to Behavioral Science." In R. W. Brislin, S. Bochner, and W. J. Lonner (Eds.), *Cross-Cultural Perspectives on Learning.* Beverly Hills, Calif.: Sage, 1975.

Rosch, E. "Universals and Culture Specifics in Human Categorization." In R. W. Brislin, S. Bochner, and W. J. Conner (Eds.), *Cross-Cultural Perspectives on Learning.* New York: Wiley, 1975.

Salili, F., Maehr, M. L., and Fyans, L. J., Jr. "Evaluating Morality and Achievement: A Study of the Interaction of Social, Cultural, and Developmental Trends." *International Journal of Intercultural Relations,* 1981, *5* (2), 147–163.

Schaie, K. W. "A General Model for the Study of Developmental Problems." *Psychological Bulletin,* 1965, *64,* 843–861.

Schaie, K. W., and Strother, C. R. "A Cross-Sequential Study of Age Change on Cognitive Behavior." *Psychological Bulletin,* 1968, *70,* 671–680.

Shigemasu, K. "Development and Validation of a Simplified M Group Regression Model." *Journal of Educational Statistics,* 1976, *3,* 157–180.

Singer, M. "A Survey of Culture and Personality Theory and Research." In B. Kaplan (Ed.), *Studying Personality Cross-Culturally.* Evanston, Ill.: Row, Peterson, 1961.

Sprague, R., Maehr, M. L., and Fyans, L. J., Jr. "The Cross-National Analysis of Childhood Psychopathology." Paper presented at the American College of Neuropsychiatry, San Juan, Puerto Rico, December 1981.

Tanter, R. "Toward a Theory of Political Development." In R. Naroll and R. Cohen (Eds.), *A Handbook on Method in Cultural Anthropology.* New York: Columbia University Press, 1973.

Triandis, H. C. *The Analysis of Subjective Culture.* New York: Wiley, 1972.

Triandis, H. C. "Culture Training, Cognitive Complexity, and Interpersonal Attitudes." In R. W. Brislin, S. Bochner, and W. J. Lonner (Eds.), *Cross-Cultural Perspectives on Learning.* New York: Wiley, 1975.

Turner, M. B. *Philosophy and the Science of Behavior.* New York: Appleton-Century-Crofts, 1967.

Winer, B. J. *Statistical Principles in Experimental Design.* New York: McGraw-Hill, 1971.

Winkler, R. A. *Introduction to Bayesian Inference and Decision.* New York: Holt, Rinehart and Winston, 1972.

Zellner, A. *An Introduction to Bayesian Inference in Econometrics.* New York: Wiley, 1971.

Leslie J. Fyans, Jr., is research psychologist and psychometrician of the testing and assessment program of the Illinois State Board of Education, Springfield.

Understanding a profile of scores in light of the covariation among universe scores and among errors of measurement is crucial.

Multivariate Generalizability Theory

Noreen M. Webb
Richard J. Shavelson
Ebrahim Maddahian

Educational and psychological measurements often provide multiple scores describing, for example, individuals' intellectual functioning, academic achievement and personality. Often when each score is interpreted by itself, occasions arise in which patterns or profiles of scores and score composites are also interpreted. For example, particular patterns of scores on the Wechsler Intelligence Scale for Children are used to place students in special education programs; a composite of these scores provides an IQ index. In assessing the reliability of such measurements, most studies take a univariate approach. The most common procedure is to determine the reliability of each subtest separately. Another method, sometimes used in generalizability studies, is to determine the generalizability of a particular composite of subtests. Neither method, however, assesses sources of error covariation among the multiple scores. Such information is important for designing an optimal decision study and for permitting a decision maker to determine the composite with maximum generalizability. For these purposes, multivariate analysis is most appropriate.

L. J. Fyans, Jr. (Ed.). *Generalizability Theory: Inferences and Practical Applications.*
New Directions for Testing and Measurement, no. 18. San Francisco: Jossey-Bass, June 1983.

In this chapter, we present some aspects of multivariate generalizability theory. Just as univariate generalizability theory stresses interpretation of the pattern of variance components, we stress interpretation of variance and covariance components. We also provide a summary index for a composite of subtest scores, a multivariate generalizability coefficient analogous to the univariate coefficient. In order to make the presentation concrete, we use three mathematical subtests from the Beginning Teacher Evaluation Study (Fisher and others, 1978).

The Beginning Teacher Evaluation Study

In 1972, the California Commission for Teacher Preparation and Licensing and the National Institute of Education mounted an eight-year research program called the Beginning Teacher Evaluation Study (BTES) to identify effective teaching behavior in elementary school reading and mathematics. To explore the impact of teaching on student learning, the study related student and teacher behavior variables to student achievement. For example, student achievement was predicted from the amount of time that a student attended to instructional activities during a lesson, the amount of time that a teacher allocated to instructional activities, and the frequency with which a teacher provided students with feedback about the accuracy of their work.

To assess student achievement, test batteries were developed in reading and mathematics; each battery had at least ten subtests. Most analyses related student and teacher behavior to scores on each subtest or to scores on pairs of subtests matched for content. A few analyses used the total test score, equal to the sum of all subtest scores in a battery. (For a description of the BTES, see Fisher and others, 1978). Three subtests representing basic computational skills were selected from the mathematics test battery at grade 5: addition and subtraction (addition and subtraction of two- to four-digit numbers), multiplication (multiplication of one- to five-digit numbers), and properties and factors (hereafter called *division* — inverse relationships among numbers and factors of numbers). These subtests can be interpreted separately as measures of individual mathematical skills, or they can be interpreted as a profile that gives evidence of hierarchical dependence among these skills. In the latter case, division requires addition, subtraction, and multiplication, while multiplication requires addition skills.

Estimation of Variance and Covariance Components

Perhaps the easiest way to describe the multivariate version of generalizability theory is by analogy to the univariate case. (We assume that the reader is familiar with the univariate case of generalizability theory. Chapter One in this volume, Cronbach and others (1972), and Shavelson and Webb

(1981) all describe it.) In the univariate case, an observed score is decomposed into the universe score and error scores corresponding to multiple, independent sources of error variation. An estimate of each component of variation in the observed score is obtained, usually with the algebraic machinery of the analysis of variance. For example, assume that fifth-grade students (p) received the three math subtests (s) on two different occasions (o). For this two-facet crossed design, in which p represents a sample of students, and s and o represent the facets of measurement, subtests and occasions respectively, $\sigma^2{}_p$ is the estimated universe score variance. For relative decisions, when an individual's score is used to compare the individual with a peer group, the estimate of the multifaceted error variance is

$$
(1) \qquad \hat{\sigma}^2_\delta = \frac{\hat{\sigma}^2_{ps}}{n'_s} + \frac{\hat{\sigma}^2_{po}}{n'_o} + \frac{\hat{\sigma}^2_{pso,e}}{n'_s n'_o}
$$

where n'_s and n'_o are the numbers of levels of the facets in the decision study, and the generalizability coefficient is

$$
(2) \qquad \hat{\varrho}^2 = \frac{\hat{\sigma}^2_p}{\hat{\sigma}^2_p + \hat{\sigma}^2_\delta}
$$

In extending the notion of multifaceted error variance from generalizability theory to multivariate designs, we treat subtest not as a facet of measurement but as three dependent variables: addition and subtraction $(_aX_{po})$, multiplication $(_mX_{po})$, and division $(_dX_{po})$. For each measure, the components of the observed score variance (σ^2_x) reflect variation between students (σ^2_p) and a residual, which is the interaction of students with occasions confounded with error $(\sigma^2_{po,e})$:

$$
(3a) \qquad \sigma^2(_aX_{po}) = \sigma^2(_ap) + \sigma^2(_apo,e)
$$

$$
(3b) \qquad \sigma^2(_mX_{po}) = \sigma^2(_mp) + \sigma^2(_mpo,e)
$$

$$
(3c) \qquad \sigma^2(_dX_{po}) = \sigma^2(_dp) + \sigma^2(_dpo,e)
$$

where a is the addition and subtraction subtest, m is the multiplication subtest, d is the division subtest, X is an observed score, p is persons, and o is occasions. So, $\sigma^2(_aX_{po})$ is the observed score variance on the addition and subtraction subtest, while $\sigma^2(_dpo,e)$ is the residual variance on the division subtest. Moreover, the components of one score (for example, $_aX_{po}$) can be related to the components of the other scores (for example, $_mX_{po}$). For a composite of these three scores, the expected observed score variances, the universe score variance, and the residual variance depend on the components of covariance as well as on the components of variance. We express the observed score variance of this composite as a variance-covariance matrix:

(4)
$$\begin{pmatrix} \sigma^2(_aX_{po}) & \sigma(_aX_{po},\,_mX_{po}) & \sigma(_aX_{po},\,_dX_{po}) \\ \sigma(_aX_{po},\,_mX_{po}) & \sigma^2(_mX_{po})\sigma(_mX_{po},\,_dX_{po}) \\ \sigma(_aX_{po},\,_dX_{po}) & \sigma(_mX_{po},\,_dX_{po}) & \sigma^2(_dX_{po}) \end{pmatrix}$$

where the variances are defined as earlier and $\sigma(_aX_{po},\,_mX_{po})$ is the covariance between scores on the addition and subtraction and multiplication subtests, $\sigma(_aX_{po},\,_dX_{po})$ is the covariance between scores on the addition and subtraction and multiplication subtests, and $\sigma(_mX_{po},\,_dX_{po})$ is the covariance between scores on the multiplication and division subtests. The expected observed score variance can be decomposed into components for universe score variance and error variances. The expected observed score variance-covariance matrix can also be decomposed. For relative decisions, this decomposition is

(4a)
$$= \begin{pmatrix} \sigma^2(_ap) & \sigma(_ap,\,_mp) & \sigma(_ap,\,_dp) \\ \sigma(_ap,\,_mp) & \sigma^2(_mp) & \sigma(_mp,\,_dp) \\ \sigma(_ap,\,_dp) & \sigma(_mp,\,_dp)\sigma^2(_dp) \end{pmatrix}$$
$$+$$
$$\begin{pmatrix} \sigma^2(_aRES) & \sigma(_aRES,\,_mRES) & \sigma(_aRES,\,_dRES) \\ \sigma(_aRES,\,_mRES) & \sigma^2(_mRES) & \sigma(_mRES,\,_dRES) \\ \sigma(_aRES,\,_dRES) & \sigma(_mRES,\,_dRES) & \sigma^2(_dRES) \end{pmatrix}$$

Just as analysis of variance can be used to obtain estimated components of variance, multivariate analysis of variance provides a computational procedure for obtaining estimated components of variance and covariance. While analysis of variance provides scalar values for the sums of squares and mean squares, multivariate analysis of variance provides matrices of sums of squares and cross products (SSCP) and mean squares and cross products (MSCP).

Estimates of the components of covariance are obtained by setting the expected mean product (MP) equations equal to the observed mean products and solving the set of simultaneous equations. (In the univariate case, estimated variance components are obtained by setting the expected mean square equations equal to the observed mean squares and solving the set of simultaneous equations.) The equations that follow relate mean products to their expectations such that components of variance and covariance for the universe score matrix in equation 4a can be obtained:

(5)
$$MS(_ap) = \sigma^2(_aRES) + n_o\sigma^2(_ap)$$
$$MS(_mp) = \sigma^2(_mRES) + n_o\sigma^2(_mp)$$
$$MS(_dp) = \sigma^2(_dRES) + n_o\sigma^2(_dp)$$
$$MP(_ap,\,_mp) = \sigma(_aRES,\,_mRES) + n_o\sigma(_ap,\,_mp)$$
$$MP(_ap,\,_dp) = \sigma(_aRES,\,_dRES) + n_o\sigma(_ap,\,_dp)$$
$$MP(_mp,\,_dp) = \sigma(_mRES,\,_dRES) + n_o\sigma(_mp,\,_dp)$$

The first three equations reflect the univariate case, in which each subtest is examined separately, whereas all six equations represent the multivariate case.

In the Beginning Teacher Evaluation Study, a high component of covariance for the addition and subtraction and multiplication universe scores relative to the residual component of covariance indicates that students with high scores on the addition and subtraction subtest tend to have high scores on the multiplication subtest. A high component of covariance for the residual suggests that unexplained factors undermine the stability of scores from one occasion to the next and that this instability contributes to both the addition and subtraction and the multiplication subtest scores.

Multivariate Generalizability Coefficients and Canonical Variates

Joe and Woodward (1976) have extended the univariate generalizability coefficient of Cronbach and others (1972) to a multivariate coefficient. From a random effects multivariate analysis of variance, the canonical variates are determined to maximize the ratio of universe score variation to universe score plus error variation. For the one-facet crossed design, Joe and Woodward's multivariate coefficient is

$$(6) \qquad \varrho^2 = \frac{\underline{a}'V_p\underline{a}}{\underline{a}'V_p\underline{a} + \dfrac{\underline{a}'V_{po,e}\underline{a}}{n'_o}}$$

where V is a matrix of variance and covariance components estimated from mean products matrices, n'_o is the number of conditions of facet o in a D study, and $\underline{a}$ is the vector of canonical coefficients that maximizes the ratio of universe-score variation to universe-score plus error variation.

For any design, $\hat{\varrho}^2$ and $\underline{a}$ can be obtained by solving the following set of equations:

$$(7) \qquad [V_p - \varrho_s^2(V_p + V_\delta)]\underline{a} = \underline{0}$$

where the subscript s refers to the $r(s = 1, \ldots, 4)$ characteristic roots of (7) and V_δ is the multivariate analogue to σ_δ^2. For each multivariate generalizability coefficient corresponding to a characteristic root in equation 7, a set of canonical coefficients defines a composite of the scores. The number of composites defined by a multivariate generalizability analysis is equal to the number of different measures entered into the analysis. By definition, the first composite is the most reliable.

The analyses that follow illustrate the estimation of components of variance and covariance, univariate and multivariate generalizability coefficients, and canonical coefficients defining the composites.

Design. One hundred and twenty-seven fifth-grade students completed the three mathematics subtests on two occasions approximately six weeks apart during the first quarter of the school year. The number of items in each subtest ranged between ten and eighteen. To obtain a balanced design with an equal number of items in each subtest, ten items were selected at random from each subtest and the three subtest total scores were used as the vector of dependent variables in the multivariate analysis.

A balanced design was preferred to an unbalanced design for two reasons. First, the computational procedures for obtaining variance components in unbalanced designs are complex and require large amounts of region in computer programs. Second, in a comparison of balanced and unbalanced designs for a multifaceted data set, Shavelson and Webb (1981) found similar variance components and generalizability coefficients across designs. By using subtest scores, we ignored items as a facet. For a multivariate treatment of test scores that explicitly takes into account the item facet, see the chapter by Brennan in this volume.

For the multivariate generalizability analysis, a random effects multivariate analysis of variance was fitted to the data from the addition and subtraction, multiplication, and division scores. The design crossed persons (p) with occasions (o). Because the focus of the BTES was on prediction and hence on individual differences between persons, the variance component matrix for persons (Vp) is interpreted as universe score variation and covariation, and we are concerned with relative decisions. Thus, in this study measurement error consists of the components of variance and covariance for the interaction between persons and occasions $(V_{po,e})$. Variance component matrices were computed from the mean square matrices. For this analysis, the matrices of variance components, coefficients of generalizability, and canonical weights corresponding to each coefficient of generalizability were computed.

The technical details of the data analyses are presented in the appendix, which includes computational procedures for computing the mean squares and cross products; the input into SAS MATRIC; variance component matrices, coefficients of generalizability, and canonical weights from the sum of squares and cross products; and the resulting output.

Multivariate Generalizability. In order to estimate the components of variance and covariance (equation 5), we use the sums of squares and cross product matrices and the mean squares and cross product matrices depicted in Table 1. The first entry in Table 1 corresponds to the persons source of variance. It is a matrix, with sums of squares on the main diagonal and sums of cross products on the sides. The matrix of mean squares and cross products is simply the sums of squares and cross products divided by their corresponding degrees of freedom. The entries in the remaining mean squares and cross product matrices are obtained in the same way.

The estimated covariance component matrices representing the three sources of variation in the design—persons, occasions, and the residual—

Table 1. Sums of Squares and Mean Square Matrices for Multivariate Generalizability Study of Basic Skills

Source of Variation		Sums of Squares and Cross Products			Degrees of Freedom	Mean Squares and Cross Products		
		Addition and Subtraction (1)	Multiplication (2)	Division (3)		Addition and Subtraction (1)	Multiplication (2)	Division (3)
Persons (p)	(1)	867.75	629.21	270.54	126	6.89	4.99	2.15
	(2)	629.21	2157.88	641.74		4.99	17.13	5.09
	(3)	270.54	641.74	1125.36		2.15	5.09	8.93
Occasions (o)	(1)	1.28	− 14.60	− 5.46	1	1.28	− 14.60	− 5.46
	(2)	− 14.60	167.07	62.45		− 14.60	167.07	62.45
	(3)	− 5.46	62.45	23.34		− 5.46	62.45	23.34
po, e	(1)	294.72	106.10	0.46	126	2.34	0.84	0.00
	(2)	106.10	735.93	35.05		0.84	5.84	0.28
	(3)	0.46	35.05	219.16		0.00	0.28	1.74

appear in Table 2. In all parts of Table 2, the variance components are estimated in the usual way, namely by setting the expected mean squares equal to the observed mean squares and solving the set of simultaneous equations. (See Chapter One in this sourcebook.) Calculation of the estimated components of covariance is analogous to the calculation of variance components. We need only to replace the variances in the expected mean squares equation with the appropriate covariances. For example, to determine the expected covariances for the person source, we replace the variances in the equation for expected mean squares — for example, $MS(p) = \sigma^2(res) + n_o\sigma^2(p)$ — with the corresponding covariances–mean crossproduct $= \sigma(_a res, \ _m res) + n_o\sigma(_a p, \ _m p)$ — and solve:

$$4.99 = 0.84 + 2\sigma(_a p, \ _m p)$$
$$\sigma(_a p, \ _m p) = 2.08$$

The other covariance components in Table 2 are solved in analogous fashion. In Table 2, only the components for one occasion are included. To obtain the results for multiple occasions, the components corresponding to the residual (po, e) need only to be divided by the number of occasions.

The components of covariance in the multivariate analysis provide new information. The moderately large components of covariance for persons (ranging between 1.07 and 2.41) reflect the underlying positive correlations among the subtests. Students who score well on the addition and subtraction subtest also tend to score well on the multiplication and division subtests. The relatively small component of covariance between addition and subtraction and division suggests, however, that the relationship between universe scores

Table 2. Estimated Variance and Covariance Components for Multivariate Generalizability Study of Basic Skills ($n_o = 1$)

Source of Variation		Addition and Subtraction (1)	Multiplication (2)	Division (3)
Persons (p)	(1)	2.27		
	(2)	2.08	5.64	
	(3)	1.07	2.41	3.60
Occasions (o)	(1)	.00		
	(2)	– .12	1.27	
	(3)	– .04	.49	.17
po, e[a]	(1)	2.34		
	(2)	.84	5.84	
	(3)	.00	.28	1.74

[a]Effect contributing to measurement error.

on these two subtests is weaker than the relationship between universe scores on these subtests and multiplication. From a substantive perspective, this finding is important. We can interpret it as meaning that division requires addition, subtraction, and multiplication, while multiplication requires only addition.

The matrix of variance and covariance components for persons is one of the most important pieces of information generated by multivariate generalizability analysis. Because the covariance components are estimates of the covariation between universe scores, they help us to interpret the separate subtest scores, and they show whether it is reasonable to form a composite of the scores. The substantial covariation among the three subtests in the study described here shows that it is reasonable to consider the three subtests as representing an underlying dimension of basic skills; consequently, a composite of the scores is interpretable.

The components of covariance for the residual reflect measurement error, here the person-by-occasion interaction, and unexplained covariation. The largest covariance component (.84) is that between addition and subtraction and multiplication. To the extent that the effect for the person-by-occasion interaction contributes to this component, we can infer not only that students are rank ordered differently across occasions but that the differences are consistent across the two subtests. For example, persons who score high in addition and subtraction will have the same pattern of scores in multiplication. To the extent that this component is due to unexplained variation, the unexplained factors that contribute to the variation in test scores also contribute to the covariation between scores. The zero covariance component between addition and subtraction and division indicates that the inconsistent rank ordering of persons across occasions on one subtest is not related to the inconsistency on the other subtest. For example, persons who score better in addition and subtraction relative to others on one occasion than on another do not necessarily have the same pattern of scores in division.

The results just described for universe score and error variation and covariation point to the possibility that interpretations of observed correlations may yield misleading conclusions about the relationships among the universe scores. (Compare correction for attenuation in classical test theory.) Because the observed variances and covariances are the sum of universe score and error variances and covariances (see equation 4), the observed correlations can be quite different from the universe score correlations. In the study described here, the observed correlations underestimate the correlations among universe scores. The observed correlations among subtest scores (calculated using the sum of universe score and error variance and covariance components in Table 2 as the observed variances and covariances; see equation 4) range between .22 and .40, whereas the correlations of universe scores (calculated using the universe score variance and covariance components in Table 2) range between

.37 and .58. The discrepancy between observed and universe score correlations depends on the pattern of error variances and covariances. In the current example, zero or negative covariance components for error would have produced small observed correlations among the subtest scores.

The information about universe score and error covariation can also be used to obtain the dimensions of mathematical skill that have maximum generalizability. These dimensions are presented in Table 3. The canonical coefficients (g in equations 6 and 7) and coefficients of generalizability are given for each dimension. The analogy of factor analysis is helpful in understanding how to interpret the canonical coefficients of the composites and the resulting dimensions. A factor analysis of a collection of variables produces several factors or dimensions. Each variable is assigned a loading on each factor. The factor loadings show the degree to which each variable is related to the factor. They also help to define the meaning of the factor. The canonical coefficients (g) in the multivariate generalizability analysis are analogous to factor loadings, the dimensions are analogous to factors, and the composites are analogous to factor scores.

When the generalizability of mathematics scores was estimated for a single occasion, one dimension with generalizability coefficient exceeding .60 emerged from the analysis. That dimension was a general composite heavily weighted by division; it had a generalizability coefficient of .71. Analysis with two raters produced two dimensions with generalizability coefficients exceeding .60. The first is the general composite described earlier; it has a generalizability coefficient of .83. The second is a contrast between addition and subtraction and division; it has a generalizability coefficient of .61.

Discussion

The multivariate analyses of mathematics skills described here provided information that cannot be obtained in a univariate analysis, namely information about facets that contribute to covariance among scores. The covariance components for persons showed substantial universe covariation among the

Table 3. Canonical Variates for Multivariate Generalizability Study of Basic Skills

	Canonical Coefficients					
	$n_0 = 1$			$n_0 = 2$		
	I	*II*	*III*	*I*	*II*	*III*
(1) Addition and Subtraction	.11	− .36	− .34	.11	− .42	− .42
(2) Multiplication	.07	− .11	.31	.07	− .13	.38
(3) Division	.35	.28	− .12	.37	.33	− .15
Coefficient of Generalizability (ϱ^2)	.71	.44	.33	.83	.61	.50

subtests, which provides support for the hypothesis that the subtest scores represent an underlying dimension of basic skills. The covariance components for error—here, the interaction between occasions and persons and unexplained sources of variation—showed that error contributed to the observed covariances as well as the observed variances. Furthermore, the decomposition of observed variances and covariances showed that the observed correlations among the subtests underestimated the true correlations. In general, the discrepancy between observed and true correlations is the greatest when error variances are large and error covariances are small or negative. Only by examining patterns of universe score and error variation and covariation can we determine the discrepancy between the observed and error-free relationships among scores.

In order to further understand the multivariate analysis, it is helpful to compare the results of the multivariate analysis to those of univariate analyses. We estimated generalizability coefficients for each subtest using a person × occasions design. The multivariate analysis produced a reliable composite of scores whose coefficient of generalizability (.83) was larger than the coefficients of the univariate analyses of the individual mathematical skills (.66 to .80) but not much larger than the generalizability coefficient of the sum of the scores in the univariate analysis (.81). In general, we can expect the weights of the subtest scores and the generalizability coefficients of the separate univariate analyses, the univariate analysis of the sum of the scores, and the multivariate analysis to converge under two conditions. The first and trivial case occurs when the scores are uncorrelated. A multivariate generalizability analysis will produce results identical to the results of a series of univariate analyses; each canonical variate is represented by one score, and the generalizability of the variates corresponds to the generalizability of the univariate analyses. The univariate analysis of the sum of the scores yields a coefficient between the lowest and highest coefficients of the separate univariate analyses, but it is not meaningful, because the scores in the composite reflect different, unrelated dimensions.

The second case occurs when the scores are highly correlated. In that case, separate univariate analyses produce nearly identical generalizability coefficients. Multivariate analysis produces a composite with a generalizability coefficient equal to those of the separate univariate analyses; all scores in the composite have equal weights. The multivariate generalizability coefficient is also nearly equal to the coefficient of the univariate analysis of the sum of the scores (a composite with weights equal to one) when the correlations among scores have intermediate values. The generalizability coefficients will depend on the patterns of error variances and the magnitudes of the correlations among the scores.

One issue in the interpretation of results of multivariate analysis concerns the weights in canonical variates. In multivariate analysis, the data, not the investigators, define the composites of maximum generalizability. When composites are defined a priori by theory (for example, by a theory of human abilities) or practice (for example, by interpretation of subtests for classification), either univariate or multivariate generalizability procedures can be used to determine the generalizability of the composite. In univariate analysis, the composite of scores can be calculated, and entered into the analysis. In multivariate analysis, the weights determined a priori can be entered directly into equation 6 as the a vector. Although the univariate and multivariate analyses produce identical generalizability coefficients in this case, the multivariate analysis yields additional information about the sources of universe and error covariation among the scores, as described earlier. Such information is important for designing optimal decision studies.

Although multivariate generalizability analysis seems to be a powerful tool for assessing the reliability of multiple dependent measures, some problems need to be addressed. The well-known problems concerning the sampling variability of estimated variance components, such as wide confidence intervals with moderate sample sizes, negative estimates, and computational complexity in unbalanced designs (Calkins and others, 1978; Leone and Nelson, 1966; Lindquist, 1963; Shavelson and Webb, 1981; Smith, 1978) probably extend to the estimation of components of covariance. Although Woodward and Joe (1973) address the problem of how to allocate measurements (for example n_i and n_j) to reduce the sampling variability of estimated variance components, Joe and Woodward (1976) point out that the sampling variability of the multivariate generalizability coefficient has yet to be investigated. Furthermore, the sampling variability of canonical coefficients that define the dimensions of maximum generalizability needs to be investigated.

Appendix: Computational Procedures

Computations were performed using the Biomedial Computer Programs-Version P (*BMDP Statistical Software*, 1981) and the Statistical Analysis System (SAS Institute, 1979). Variance components in the univariate analyses were computed using the BMDP8V program. For the multivariate analyses, the sums of squares and cross product matrices were computed using the multivariate analysis of variance option of the General Linear Model (GLM) procedure (Figure 1). Estimation of components of variance and covariance, coefficients of generalizability, and canonical coefficients was carried out using the SAS MATRIX procedure (Figure 2).

To solve equation (7) for the canonical coefficients and coefficients of generalizability, it is necessary to compute the eigenvalues — corresponding to the coefficients of generalizability — and the eigenvectors — corresponding to the canonical coefficients defining the composite for each generalizability coefficient — of the following product of matrices: $(V_p)(V_p + V_\delta)^{-1}$. Because the MATRIX procedure computes the eigenvalues and eigenvectors only for symmetric matrices and the product of the two matrices is in general nonsymmetric, the two-matrix problem was transformed into a one-matrix problem by change of basis. The steps of this transformation are described by Bock (1975, pp. 91–92).

Figure 1. Computer Input to Obtain Coefficients for One Occasion

```
 1              PROC MATRIX;
 2              SSP=
 3                867.7480     629.2087    270.5354/
 4                629.2087    2157.8319    641.7441/
 5                270.5354     641.7441   1125.3622;
 6              MSP=SSP#/126;
 7              SSO=
 8                  1.2756     -14.5984     -5.4569/
 9                -14.5984     167.0709     62.4488/
10                 -5.4569      62.4488     23.3425;
11              MSO=SSO#/1;
12              SSE=
13                294.7244     106.0984      0.4567/
14                106.0984     735.9291     35.0512/
15                  0.4567      35.0512    219.1575;
16              MSE=SSE#/126;
17              VE=MSE;
18              VP=(MSP-MSE)#/2;
19              VO=(MSO-MSE)#/127;
20              TEMP=VP + VE#/1;
21              A=VP;
22              B=TEMP;
23              CBT=HALF(B);
24              CB=CBT';
25              CBINV=INV(CB);
26              CBINVT=CBINV';
27              NEW=CBINV*A*CBINVT;
28              EIGEN G TEMPWTS NEW;
29              WTS=CBINVT*TEMPWTS;
30              PRINT MSP MSO MSE VP VO VE WTS G;
```

where   SS = sums of squares and cross products matrix,

      MS = mean squares and cross products matrix,

      P = persons,

      O = occasions,

      E = residual (here, po,e),

      V = variance component matrix,

      G = multivariate generalizability coefficients, and

    WTS = canonical coefficients.

Figure 2. Computer Output

MSP	COL1	COL2	COL3
ROW1	6.88689	4.99372	2.14711
ROW2	4.99372	17.126	5.09321
ROW3	2.14711	5.09321	8.93145

MSO	COL1	COL2	COL3
ROW1	1.2756	-14.5984	-5.4569
ROW2	-14.5984	167.071	62.4488
ROW3	-5.4569	62.4488	23.3425

MSE	COL1	COL2	COL3
ROW1	2.33908	0.842051	0.0036246
ROW2	0.842051	5.84071	0.278184
ROW3	0.0036246	0.278184	1.73935

VP	COL1	COL2	COL3
ROW1	2.2739	2.07583	1.07174
ROW2	2.07583	5.64267	2.40751
ROW3	1.07174	2.40751	3.59605

VO	COL1	COL2	COL3
ROW1	-0.00837388	-0.121578	-0.0429963
ROW2	-0.121578	1.26953	0.489532
ROW3	-0.0429963	0.489532	0.170104

VE	COL1	COL2	COL3
ROW1	2.33908	0.842051	0.0036246
ROW2	0.842051	5.84071	0.278184
ROW3	0.0036246	0.278184	1.73935

WTS	COL1	COL2	COL3
ROW1	0.106638	-0.360451	-0.34526
ROW2	0.0690314	-0.107825	0.310878
ROW3	0.34681	0.230781	-0.123035

G	COL1
ROW1	0.710379
ROW2	0.443183
ROW3	0.332101

References

BMDP Statistical Software. Los Angeles: University of California Press, 1981.

Bock, R. D. *Multivariate Statistical Methods in Behavioral Research.* New York: McGraw-Hill, 1975.

Calkins, D. S., Erlich, O., Marston, P. T., and Malitz, P. "An Empirical Investigation of the Distributions of Generalizability Coefficients and Variance Estimates for an Application of Generalizability Theory." Paper presented at the annual meeting of the American Educational Research Association, Toronto, March 1978.

Cronbach, L. J., Gleser, G. C., Nanda, H., and Rajaratnam, N. *The Dependability of Behavioral Measurements: Theory of Generalizability for Scores and Profiles.* New York: Holt, Rinehart and Winston, 1972.

Fisher, C. W., Filby, N. N., Marliave, R., Cahen, L. S., Dishaw, M. M., Moore, J. E., and Berliner, D. C. *Teaching Behaviors, Academic Learning Time, and Student Achievement: Final Report of Phase III-B, Beginning Teacher Evaluation Study.* Technical Report V-1, San Francisco: Far West Laboratory for Educational Research and Development, 1978.

Joe, G. W., and Woodward, J. A. "Some Developments in Multivariate Generalizability." *Psychometrika,* 1976, *41,* 205–217.

Leone, F. C., and Nelson, L. S. "Sampling Distributions of Variance Components I: Empirical Studies of Balanced Nested Designs." *Technometrics,* 1966, *8,* 457–568.

Lindquist, E. F. *Design and Analysis of Experiments in Psychology and Education.* Boston: Houghton Mifflin, 1963.

SAS Institute. *SAS User's Guide.* Raleigh, N.C.: SAS Institute, 1979.

Shavelson, R. J., and Webb, N. M. "Generalizability Theory: 1973–1980." *British Journal of Mathematical and Statistical Psychology,* 1981, *34,* 133–166.

Smith, P. "Sampling Errors of Variance Components in Small Sample Multifacet Generalizability Studies." *Journal of Educational Statistics,* 1978, *3,* 319–346.

Woodward, J. A., and Joe, G. W. "Maximizing the Coefficients of Generalizability in Multi-Facet Decision Studies." *Psychometrika,* 1973, *38,* 173–181.

Noreen M. Webb is associate professor of education, University of California at Los Angeles.

Richard J. Shavelson is director of the education and human resources program at the Rand Corporation, Los Angeles, and professor of education, University of California at Los Angeles.

Ebrahim Maddahian is research associate at the Center for Health and Social Services Research, Pasadena, California.

Multivariate generalizability theory can be used to tailor psychometric models to tests developed according to a table of specifications thus bridging a gap between psychometric theory and test development practice.

Multivariate Generalizability Models for Tests Developed from Tables of Specifications

David Jarjoura
Robert L. Brennan

Given the widespread use of tables of specificiations to develop test forms, it is noteworthy that the psychometric literature has relatively little guidance for measurement specialists considering measurement properties of tests developed in this manner. Some guidance has been provided in an illustration of generalizability theory by Cronbach and others (1972), but their example employs univariate generalizability theory for a balanced design in which equal numbers of items are nested within each of several fixed strata, cells, or categories (see also Brennan, 1983). In many practical situations, however, the value of this approach is limited, because there are different numbers of items within the different cells of a table of specifications. Also, univariate analysis does not allow the researcher to examine variance and covariance components for individual cells, categories, or strata.

The principal purpose of this chapter is to illustrate a use of multivariate generalizability theory (Cronbach and others, 1972) that involves analyzing data resulting from the administration of multiple forms of a test. All the multiple forms are developed according to the same table of specifications. In the models that we consider, each examinee is administered only one

L. J. Fyans, Jr. (Ed.). *Generalizability Theory: Inferences and Practical Applications.*
New Directions for Testing and Measurement, no. 18. San Francisco: Jossey-Bass, June 1983.

form, and each examinee has as many universe scores as there are fixed categories in a table of specifications.

In our approach, the estimated variance and covariance components for categories that result from analysis of each individual form are averaged to provide estimated variance and covariance components for the measurement procedure implied by a table of specifications. These average variance and covariance components are especially informative in evaluating characteristics of the measurement procedure itself, as opposed to the specific characteristics of a particular form.

Here, we will not attach great importance to the characteristics of particular forms, because the context that we consider is one in which new forms of a test are constantly being developed, equated, and used in an operational testing program. Consider, for example, the American College Testing Assessment Program (AAP), which contains four cognitive subtests, each of which can be described in terms of a table of specifications (American College Testing Program, 1980). During any testing year, an examinee will take one of several different forms of the AAP. In the usual course of events, neither the examinee nor a decision maker will pay attention to the specific characteristics of the particular form. Furthermore, during any given year, several new forms of the AAP are being developed for use in subsequent years. For these reasons, the characteristics of the measurement procedures implied by the tables of specifications for the subtests are our principal concern; to put it another way, we want to characterize the AAP, not particular forms of the AAP. Clearly, our analyses must be based on data from forms that have already been used, but our results can be generalized to new forms, since the same tables of specifications are used to develop both old forms and new forms.

Our emphasis on the actual use of multiple test forms is one important feature of the approach that we take to modeling data from tests developed according to a table of specifications. Another feature of our approach is the importance that it accords to composite universe scores, which are defined as a weighted sum of universe scores for the fixed categories in a table of specifications. For most tests developed according to a table of specifications, the only score reported to examinees and decision makers is an observed score over all items in the test or some transformation of it (for example, a transformation resulting from an equating procedure). Under these circumstances, the error variances of principal interest are those involving differences between composite universe scores across strata and estimates of such composite universe scores. For this reason, we give considerable attention in this chapter to defining, estimating, and interpreting composite universe scores and various error variances associated with estimating them. Among other things, we show that it is possible to study the contributions that categories make to composite universe score variance and error variances. Also, our approach enables an investigator to examine what happens to mean-squared error when a test form deviates from a table of specifications.

In the next section, we present a model in which the universe consists of different sets of items, each of which is nested within one of C fixed categories of a table of specifications; thus, for this model, items constitute the only random facet in the universe of generalization. We use data from eight forms of the Mathematics subtest of the AAP to illustrate applying this model to a frequently encountered type of measurement procedure. Other treatments of this model are provided by Brennan (1983) and Jarjoura and Brennan (1981, 1982). Multivariate generalizability models can also be developed for more complicated tables of specifications. For example, Jarjoura (1981) treats a model for the English Usage subtest of the AAP in which each item is classified into one fixed category (skill) and one random category (reading passage) with different numbers of items in the categories. Among other things, treating the model for English Usage involves considering one type of correlated measurement error.

Model for a Case in Which Items Are Associated with Fixed Categories

Consider a situation in which there are C fixed categories of items in a table of specifications. In each of these categories, a certain number of items is specified; say I_c *items in category* c. The total number of items in the test is $I_+ = \sum_c I_c$. The following sampling model is used for potential item-level observations on a potential test form:

(1)
$$Y_{pci} = \mu_c + \pi_{pc} + \iota_{i:c} + \pi\iota_{pi:c}$$

$$p = 1, \ldots, P; \ c = 1, \ldots, C; \ i = 1, \ldots, I_c$$

The variable Y_{pci} represents a potential observation for person p and item i in category c. Note that the p and i indices do not refer to any particular person or item; thus, they represent random dimensions in the model. In contrast, c refers to a particular category of items, and it is associated with a fixed dimension in the model. In the illustration presented later in this section, the table of specifications consists of a single fixed dimension. Sometimes, however, a table of specifications has two or even more fixed dimensions. For a table that has two levels, say A and B, the model in equation 1 still applies, with c designating any one of the $C = AB$ cells.

Model Effects, Parameters, and Assumptions. The effects in the model are defined over the population of persons and C universes of items for the overall measurement procedure. The μ_c are the C category means; that is $\mu_c \equiv EY_{pci}$, where the expectation is over persons and items associated with the overall measurement procedure. The π_{pc} are universe score effects, such that for a particular person p^*, $\pi_{p^*c} \equiv E(Y_{pci} | p = p^*) - \mu_c$. The $\iota_{i:c}$ are item effects; they are defined similarly. The $\pi\iota_{pi:c}$ are residual effects that consist of person-item interaction and response error. Response error is defined to have an expectation of zero for any particular person-item combination; it refers to any effect or combination of effects that can cause a deviation from the expected score for a particular person-item combination.

Variance and covariance components are defined as expectations of certain squares and products of these effects. Again, the expectation is over the persons and items associated with the overall measurement procedure. For example universe score variance for category c is $\sigma(\pi)_{cc} \equiv E\pi_{pc}^2$, and the covariance between universe scores in different categories c and c' is $\sigma(\pi)_{cc'} = E\pi_{pc}\pi_{pc'}$.

We assume that, whatever process generates the observables in equation 1, expectations over this process of squares and products of the effects will give variance and covariance components defined for the overall measurement procedure. So, for universe score effects,

$$(2) \qquad E\pi_{pc}\pi_{pc'} = \sigma(\pi)_{cc'}, \ c, \ c' = 1, \ldots, C$$

With $c = c'$, this expectation gives universe score variance for category c. With $c \neq c'$, it gives the covariance between universe scores for categories c and c'. The set of variance and covariance components will sometimes be referred to by the matrix Σ_π. Similarly, for item effects,

$$(3) \qquad E\iota_{i:c}^2 = \sigma^2(\iota)_c, \ c = 1, \ldots, C$$

and for the residual effects,

$$(4) \qquad E\pi\iota_{pi:c}^2 = \sigma^2(\pi\iota)_c, \ c = 1, \ldots, C$$

Further, we assume that expectations of all the random effects in the model are zero and that, except for the $\pi_{pc}\pi_{pc'}$, all effects are uncorrelated. We do not assume that these expectations will hold for a particular sample of persons or items. To meet these assumptions, we need only to assume random and independent sampling of persons and items in categories and uncorrelated response errors.

Estimation of Variance and Covariance Components. Given the definitions and assumptions just stated, estimation of variance and covariance components can be accomplished using mean squares and products of the observations. Beyond assuming that $I_c \geq 2$ for all c, nothing else is required for the unbiased estimators provided later in this chapter.

To estimate the $\sigma^2(\iota)_c$ and $\sigma^2(\pi\iota)_c$ for any particular form, we make use of the fact that the observations for each category in a table of specifications can be associated with a $p \times i$ design. Therefore, for any category c, we use the usual estimators for the item and residual variance components for a $p \times i$ design, namely $\sigma^2(\iota)_c = [MS(i)_c - MS(pi)_c]/P, \ c = 1, \ldots, C$ and $\sigma^2(\pi\iota)_c = MS(pi)_c, \ c = 1, \ldots, C.$

To estimate Σ_π with typical element $\sigma(\pi)_{cc'}$, we use the variance-covariance matrix of category mean scores with typical element

$$s_{cc'} = \sum_{p}^{P} (Y_{pc\cdot} - Y_{\cdot c\cdot}) (Y_{pc'\cdot} - Y_{\cdot c'\cdot})/(P-1)$$

$$c, c' = 1, \ldots, C$$

where $Y_{pc\cdot} = \Sigma_i^{I_c} Y_{pci}/I_c$, and $Y_{\cdot c\cdot} = \Sigma_p^P Y_{pc\cdot}/P$. Estimators of the covariance components in Σ_π are $\hat{\sigma}(\pi)_{cc'} = s_{cc'}$ for $c \neq c'$, $(c, c' = 1, \ldots, C)$, and estimators of the variance components in Σ_π are $\hat{\sigma}(\pi)_{cc} = s_{cc} - \hat{\sigma}^2(\pi\iota)_c/I_c$, $c = 1, \ldots, C$. Finally, estimators of the μ_c for a particular form are $\hat{\mu}_c = Y_{\cdot c\cdot}$ for $c = 1, \ldots, C$.

As already noted, we do not attach great importance to the characteristics of the particular form. Therefore, we use the equations just given to obtain estimates for each of several forms; then, we obtain the average of these estimates over the several forms.

An Illustrative Example. As an example, consider the Mathematics subtest (Math) of the AAP. Generation of multiple forms of Math involves the use of a table of specifications with fixed categories of items. Thus, Math can be described by the model just given. Each of the forty items of Math falls into one of five major categories: arithmetic and algebraic operations (AAO), arithmetic and algebraic reasoning (AAR), geometry (GEO), intermediate algebra (IA), and number and numeration concepts and other advanced topics (NA). The number of items in each category is four, fourteen, eight, eight, and six, respectively. This pattern has been constant for all recent forms. The reader should note that this represents only a major categorization of the items, since more detailed categories are used in the actual table of specifications.

Table 1 provides estimates of variance and covariance components and means for Math based on eight recent forms of the test. Each form was administered to independent samples of examinees. Since each parameter was estimated for each form and since these estimates were averaged across forms, it was convenient to estimate standard errors as the standard deviation of the estimates divided by the square root of eight. These are displayed in italics in Table 1. These estimated standard errors do not require any assumptions beyond those already discussed. That is one advantage of using multiple test forms. If there were only one form, standard errors could still be estimated, but most procedures for doing so require additional assumptions (Brennan, 1983).

In $\hat{\Sigma}_\pi$, we have estimates of the universe score variances and covariances for the five categories. These estimates make it clear that there are high correlations among universe scores for different categories. The average of the

Table 1. Estimates of Variance and Covariance Components and Category Means for Math

	AAO	AAR	GEO	IA	NA
$\hat{\Sigma}_\pi$	.052 *.004*		Symmetric		
	.039 *.001*	.038 *.002*			
	.040 *.001*	.037 *.002*	.041 *.002*		
	.043 *.003*	.036 *.003*	.039 *.003*	.042 *.005*	
	.041 *.002*	.035 *.002*	.037 *.002*	.038 *.003*	.035 *.004*
$\hat{\sigma}^2(\iota)_c$	.013 *.004*	.027 *.003*	.021 *.002*	.022 *.003*	.022 *.003*
$\hat{\sigma}^2(\pi\iota)_c$	.176 *.004*	.185 *.003*	.187 *.002*	.183 *.003*	.187 *.003*
$\hat{\mu}_c$	.607 *.014*	.501 *.020*	.456 *.012*	.446 *.018*	.501 *.017*

Source: Jarjoura and Brennan (1982)

universe score correlations calculated from $\hat{\Sigma}_\pi$ is .93. The highest correlation (IA with NA) is .97, while the lowest (AAO with AAR) is .88. Generally, universe scores for NA have the highest correlation with other categories, while those for AAO have the lowest. In terms of the relative size of universe score variances, AAO appears to have a larger variance than the other categories do. Finding a category on which universe scores vary less — or more — than they do on others could influence considerations of future changes in the table of specifications. Such knowledge also provides more information about the nature of the examinee population than a single estimate of universe score variance for the overall test.

From the $\hat{\sigma}^2(\iota)_c$, GEO, IA, and NA appear to have item effect variances that are close in value, while AAO and AAR appear to have lower and higher values, respectively. Since these are relative comparisons of the variances of difficulties of items in each category, they provide information about the nature of the items in these categories. From the $\hat{\sigma}^2(\pi\iota)_c$, the residual effect variances of four of the categories appear to be very close, while AAO appears to have lower residual variance. Since these components make substantial contributions to measurement error variance, comparisons among them can be quite valuable. Finally, from the $\hat{\mu}_c$, AAO appears to be an easier category, while GEO and IA appear to be more difficult.

Composite Universe Scores and Their Variance. As noted at the beginning of this chapter, for most tests developed according to a table of specifications, the scores of principal interest are examinee scores over all categories in the table. Each examinee has a universe score for each category of items $(\mu_c + \pi_{pc})$, and a composite of these category universe scores must be defined. Jarjoura and Brennan (1982) suggest using a priori proportional weights to define the composite universe score of interest:

(5)
$$\mu_{p\cdot} \equiv \sum_c w_c(\mu_c + \pi_{pc})$$

where the w_c are proportional weights (that is, their sum is unity).

To understand why we identify the w_c as a priori weights, it is helpful to reconsider the usual test development process. The steps taken in developing a table of specifications usually involve fairly explicit consideration of the relative importance of various categories of items for the intended use and interpretation of test scores. In many cases, these considerations are a principal determining factor in decisions about the number or proportion of items to be used with each category in an operational form of a test. To the extent that this rationale holds, it makes sense to define the w_c as I_c/I_+ for $c = 1, \ldots, C$. However, it sometimes occurs that the I_c/I_+ proportions are an imperfect reflection of the w_c. For example, for a particular form of a test, some practical constraint may force the test developer to use a set of I_c such that the I_c/I_+ proportions are not identical to the w_c. Also, as we show later, by allowing the w_c to be defined a priori, we can consider what would happen to various error variances if the I_c were specified for some reason other than to reflect the relative importance of the various categories. In particular, issues regarding an optimal choice of the I_c (in a sense discussed later) can be considered.

Given equation 5, the mean composite universe score is $\mu_\cdot = \sum_c w_c \mu_c$, and the variance of composite universe scores is

(6)
$$\sigma^2(\pi)_\cdot = \sum_c w_c \left[\sum_{c'} w_{c'} \sigma(\pi)_{cc'} \right]$$

The term in brackets in equation 6 is the covariance between composite universe scores and universe scores for category c. Consequently, the proportional contribution to $\sigma^2(\pi)_\cdot$ of category c is

(7)
$$v_c = w_c \sum_{c'} w_{c'} \sigma(\pi)_{cc'} / \sigma^2(\pi)_\cdot.$$

In terms of distinctions discussed by Kelley (1923) and by Wang and Stanley (1970), the v_c play the role of effective weights, while the w_c play the role of nominal weights. From equation 7, it is clear that the v_c and w_c are usually not the same. However, when they are dramatically different, we may want to reconsider whether the w_c are reasonable for the particular measurement procedure with the particular population under consideration.

For Math, the proportions of items in the five content categories are .10, .35, .20, .20, and .15 for AAO, AAR, GEO, IA, and NA, respectively. These proportions have remained constant over all recent forms, and they appear to reflect the intended relative importance of the categories for the purposes of the AAP reasonably well. Therefore, we take these proportions as the w_c. Then, using equation 6 with the estimates of $\sigma(\pi)_{cc'}$ in Table 1, we obtain an estimated composite universe score variance of $\hat{\sigma}^2(\pi). = .0380$. Using equation 7, the v_c are .11, .34, .20, .20, and .14, which are quite similar to the w_c. This suggests that no category contributes much more or less to composite universe score variance than the defined relative importance of the category.

Simple Estimators of Composite Universe Score and Associated Errors of Measurement. Under random sampling of items within categories, an unbiased estimator of composite universe score is

$$(8) \qquad \hat{\mu}_{p.} = \sum_c w_c \sum_i^{I_c} Y_{pci}/I_c$$

When the $w_c = I_c/I_+$, as they do for Math, $\hat{\mu}_{p.}$ is simply the proportion correct score for all items in a test. Given the estimator in equation 8, measurement error variance, over persons and items, can be defined as

$$(9) \qquad \sigma^2(\Delta) = E(\hat{\mu}_{p.} - \mu_{p.})^2 = \sum_c w_c^2 [\sigma^2(\iota)_c + \sigma^2(\pi\iota)_c]/I_c$$

For Math, $\hat{\sigma}^2(\Delta) = .00517$, which is 7.3 times smaller than the estimate of composite universe variance, $\hat{\sigma}^2(\pi). = .0380$. Thus, the covariance between $\hat{\mu}_{p.}$ and $\mu_{p.}$ is 7.3 times larger than the variance of the difference $\hat{\mu}_{p.} - \mu_{p.}$.

Although the sampling model for equation 1 is for a crossed design (all examinees are administered the same items in any given sample), decisions about or comparisons among examinees are made across forms. Under most circumstances, then, the error of interest is simply the difference between universe score and an estimate of that score. This might seem obvious, but the notion of a decision study in generalizability theory could cause confusion here. Specifically, with each examinee taking only one form, the sampling model for equation 1 does not represent a decision study based on a crossed design for Math.

Since $\sigma^2(\Delta)$ in equation 9 clearly depends on the I_c one might want to find integer values for the I_c (for fixed w_c and I_+) that minimize $\sigma^2(\Delta)$. Jarjoura and Brennan (1982) provide an upper bound for $\sigma^2(\Delta)$ that facilitates doing so. For Math, it appears that the I_c now used serve to minimize $\sigma^2(\Delta)$.

Let us now consider the case in which the proportion correct score over all items in a test is always used as an estimate of composite universe score, but the w_c do not necessarily correspond with the I_c/I_+. For the estimator of composite universe score

$$(10) \qquad \tilde{\mu}_{p.} = \sum_c \sum_i Y_{pci}/I_+ = \sum_c I_c Y_{pc.}/I_+$$

the mean-squared error of measurement is

$$(11) \qquad E(\tilde{\mu}_p. - \mu_p.)^2 = \sum_c \sum_{c'} (w_c - a_c)(w_{c'} - a_{c'})\sigma(\pi)_{cc'}$$

$$+ [\sum_c (w_c - a_c)(\mu_c - \mu.)]^2$$

$$+ \sum_c a_c[\sigma^2(\iota)_c + \sigma^2(\pi\iota)_c]/I_+$$

where $a_c = I_c/I_+$. Clearly, when the a_c and w_c are not identical, this mean-squared error has nonnegative contributions from universe score variances and covariances (the $\sigma(\pi)_{cc'}$) and from differences between category means and the composite mean ($\mu_c - \mu.$).

Equation 11 can be used to investigate the increase in mean-squared error over $\sigma^2(\Delta)$ in equation 9 when there are deviations from the table of specifications and when average scores are used. For example, if a Math form is generated with only AAR items (that is, I_2 is forty and all other I_c are zero), the estimated mean-squared error calculated from equation 11 is approximately 40 percent larger than the estimated $\sigma^2(\Delta)$ based on the I_c currently used for Math. Using only AAR items is not quite as extreme as it may seem, since currently these items constitute 35 percent of the Math test. Similar comparisons have been made using other categories. Most of these comparisons produced even larger increases in estimated mean-squared error. In contrast, forms with a balanced representation of items across categories (that is, all I_c have eight items) show just a 5 percent increase in estimated mean-squared error over $\hat{\sigma}^2(\Delta)$. Thus, at least some balance of items across content categories seems highly desirable for Math. The high universe score correlations among categories that were found for Math might lead some observers to consider ignoring the specified I_c. However, the results given earlier seem to indicate that these high correlations do not allow us to disregard the table of specifications.

Adjustments for Relative Difficulty. Equation 8 provides an unbiased estimate of an individual's universe score under the assumption of random sampling of items from categories. However, in the model that we are considering, each individual takes only one form of the test, and forms can differ with respect to the average difficulty of their individual items. This suggests that estimates of examinee composite universe scores can be improved if they can be adjusted for the relative difficulty of the items in a form. If such an adjustment is so precise that it introduces virtually no additional sources of error, then measurement error variance can be viewed as not including the item effect variances. Rather, measurement error variance becomes

$$(12) \qquad \sigma^2(\delta) = \sum_c w_c^2 \sigma^2(\pi\iota)_c/I_c$$

We identify this measurement error variance adjusted for relative difficulty as $\sigma^2(\delta)$, since it has a form reminiscent of the usual $\sigma^2(\delta)$ in generalizability theory. For example, with $C = 1$, equation 12 is the usual $\sigma^2(\delta)$ based on a $p \times I$ decision study design. Also, when $w_c = I_c/I_+$, equation 12 is the error variance incorporated in the coefficient of Rajaratnam and others (1965) α_s for stratified parallel tests. However, in this chapter, the rationale for $\sigma^2(\delta)$ is that it is a measurement error variance involved in estimating composite universe scores using a particular type of adjusted observed scores. That is, we are not viewing $\sigma^2(\delta)$ as an error variance involved in using observed deviation scores as estimates of universe deviation scores.

For Math, $\hat{\sigma}^2(\delta) = .00460$, which is close to $\hat{\sigma}^2(\Delta) = .00517$, reflecting the fact that the eight forms of Math used in this study are similar in difficulty, although they are not identical. It should be noted, however, that the scores reported for Math and the other subtests in the AAP are in effect adjusted for the relative difficulty of forms through an equating procedure based on the administration of forms to large random samples of examinees. (We some-what oversimplified here, because the actual reported scores for Math are standard scores involving a transformation of equated raw scores, and the equating is performed via an equipercentile procedure. Treatment of this standard score scale lies outside the scope of this chapter.) Thus, although the various forms of Math differ slightly in difficulty, there is a logical basis for paying attention to $\hat{\sigma}^2(\delta)$.

An equating procedure is only one approach to obtaining adjustments for relative difficulty. Such adjustments can result from any number of operations on the data, so it is difficult to be very explicit about the form of measurement error variance in the general case. The best linear prediction (BLP) function derived by Jarjoura (in press) takes the fixed categories of items that occur in a test like Math into consideration. This function has the form

$$(13) \qquad \dot{\mu}_{p\cdot} = \mu_{\cdot\cdot} + \sum_c \alpha_c(Y_{\cdot c\cdot} - \mu_c) + \sum_c \beta_c(Y_{pc\cdot} - Y_{\cdot c\cdot})$$

where the α_c and β_c are functions of the w_c, the I_c, and the variance and covariance components of the measurement model; $Y_{pc\cdot}$ is the pth person's observed mean for category c; and $Y_{\cdot c\cdot}$ is the mean of the $Y_{pc\cdot}$ for all persons who took the same form as the pth person. Clearly, the term involving the β_c makes an adjustment for relative difficulty by subtracting the $Y_{\cdot c\cdot}$ from each person's observed mean category scores. The term involving the α_c makes a correction to this adjustment. This correction depends primarily on the sample size P and on the size of the item effect variances divided by the I_c. The measurement error variance from the BLP function is always less than $\sigma^2(\Delta)$.

The BLP function resembles the familiar regressed score estimates discussed by Cronbach and others (1972). However, the theoretical basis is not the same. One distinction is that the BLP function only requires knowledge of the overall measurement model parameters defined earlier in this chapter, not knowledge of the regression function of the universe scores on the observables for a given test form.

The measurement error variance from the BLP function depends on the choice of the I_c. So, an optimal choice of the I_c is one that minimizes such error variance. Derivations in Woodbury and Novick (1968) can be used to calculate an inequality or lower bound on error variance among discrete choices of the I_c. For Math, the optimal choice for the I_c under the BLP function is one in which NA items are dropped from test forms and the AAO category has twice the original number of items (Jarjoura, in press). Thus, the optimal choice of the I_c under the BLP function is quite different from the optimal choice under the estimator in equation 8, $\hat{\mu}_{p\cdot}$. Even if NA items were dropped, however, the definition of composite universe score would not change, because the w_c would remain the same; only the configuration of items used to predict this score would change. An intuitive appreciation of these results for Math can be obtained by considering measurement model parameters for Math already discussed. Since the NA category shows the highest average universe correlation with other categories (.93), little information is lost if these items are dropped. Also, the AAO category has the largest estimated universe score variance, the smallest average correlation with other categories, and the smallest item effect and residual variances. These facts suggest that AAO is a useful category for minimizing measurement error variance.

Approaches to determining optimal choices for the I_c using particular statistical criteria can help us to understand the nature of a measurement procedure, and they can provide useful information to test developers about improving measurement procedures. However, strict adherence to the use of a statistical criterion in specifying the I_c ignores many other issues. For example, such results can conflict with face validity considerations. It is not our intent to suggest that such issues are necessarily less important than those associated with using some statistical criterion for choosing the I_c.

Reliabilitylike Coefficients. For measurement procedures developed according to a table of specifications, we suggest that it is highly desirable to pay attention to many statistical results, including estimates of the variance and covariance components, composite universe score variance, and various error variances. For some purposes, we may also want to examine signal-noise ratios and reliabilitylike coefficients.

In the case of Math, we have already pointed out that $\hat{\sigma}^2(\pi)\cdot/\hat{\sigma}^2(\Delta) = 7.3$ is one estimate of the relative precision of the measurement procedure. As such, this statistic is an estimated signal-noise ratio of a type discussed by Brennan and Kane (1977), and it can be transformed to a reliabilitylike coefficient $\hat{\sigma}^2(\pi)\cdot/[\hat{\sigma}^2(\pi)\cdot + \hat{\sigma}^2(\Delta)] = .88$. Similarly, using the estimated error variance that results from adjusting observed scores for the relative difficulty of test forms, the signal-noise ratio for Math is $\hat{\sigma}^2(\pi)\cdot/\hat{\sigma}^2(\delta) = 8.2$, and the associated reliabilitylike coefficient is $\hat{\sigma}^2(\pi)./[\hat{\sigma}^2(\pi). + \hat{\sigma}^2(\delta)] = .89$. The last coefficient can also be expressed as

(14)
$$\frac{\sum\limits_{c}\sum\limits_{c'} w_c w_{c'} \hat{\sigma}(\pi)_{cc'}}{\sum\limits_{c}\sum\limits_{c'} w_c w_{c'} s_{cc'}}$$

When $w_c = I_c/I_+$, equation 14 is algebraically equivalent to the coefficient of Rajaratnam and others (1965) $\hat{\alpha}_s$. Rajaratnam and others (1965) defined their coefficient $\hat{\alpha}_s$ in terms of estimates from a single form of a measurement procedure. In contrast, our estimates of variance and covariance components in equation 14 are averages over forms. Also, the development of α_s employs a different basis for defining $\sigma^2(\delta)$ than that used in arriving at our $\sigma^2(\delta)$ in equation 12. Consequently, there are conceptual differences between our formulation and that of Rajaratnam and others (1965), even though there are some algebraic equivalences.

If we disregard the content categories in Math and analyze the data for each form in terms of a random effects $p \times i$ design, the estimates of reliability-like coefficients will differ only in the third and subsequent digits. Some observers may view this fact as an argument against undertaking the work involved in conducting the type of detailed analyses outlined here. We suggest that the analyses that we outline are much more informative than any reliabilitylike index. Indeed, excessive reliance on such indices can be more misleading than informative.

Discussion

Generalizability theory is tied to considerations of the consistency of replications of a measurement procedure, such as test forms. To ensure consistency is a major purpose of a table of specifications, and multivariate generalizability models seem to provide an ideal framework for examining measurement consistency among test forms developed using a table of specifications. In practice, a certain number of items are usually specified for each category of the table. If these categories do in fact measure different aspects of whatever is of interest, keeping these numbers constant or nearly constant across forms tends to ensure that these aspects have the same weight across forms.

By defining a universe score for each fixed category of items, it becomes possible to study the nature of these categories. This is a fundamental aspect of our analyses, because it allows us to consider differences among categories in average difficulty level, variances of difficulties, universe score variances, and residual variances. Also, it gives us an opportunity to study the separation of responses in categories through calculation of universe score correlations.

For most tests that a table of specifications is used to develop, a single score over the categories is reported and used for decision making. Therefore, considerations involving composite universe scores assume considerable importance. In general, we have defined a composite universe (of generalization) score in terms of category weights that are defined a priori. For the preceding examples, the weights that we used were those implied by the actual numbers of items in categories of test forms.

Given our definition of composite universe score, we have shown that we can study the contributions that categories make to composite universe score variance and to error variances. Also, we can consider options for estimating composite universe score and optimal choices for item numbers under these options, and it becomes possible to investigate increases in mean-squared error due to deviations from the table of specifications. We have shown that gross deviations from the specified numbers of items in categories can cause relatively large increases in mean-squared error, even in the case of high universe score correlations among categories.

A Priori Weights. In our judgment, applying the logic of multivariate models to test forms developed with a prespecified table of specifications requires us to define the composite universe score in terms of a priori weights, which we identify as the w_c. In particular, we are not attracted to procedures for choosing weights that rely principally on the statistical characteristics of a particular form or particular forms of a test. For example, the procedure for choosing weights that maximize an estimated generalizability coefficient described by Joe and Woodward (1976) is much at variance with our perspective on the use of multivariate generalizability models with actual test forms based on a table of specifications. In effect, an application of the Joe and Woodward approach would provide a set of a posteriori weights that sometimes have little to do with the relative importance of categories of items for a prespecified intended use of a test.

At the same time, however, it has to be recognized that our notion of a priori weights is intimately linked with the intended use of a test. It is certainly possible for two decision makers to use the same test for different purposes that involve different degrees of emphasis for the various categories in a table of specifications. In such a case, the two investigators may properly consider and use different sets of a priori weights. Also, in the early stages of defining a universe of generalization and deciding on the relative importance of various categories, it can be both reasonable and valuable to use various statistical results to make an informed choice of the w_c. For example, a well-designed generalizability study using relatively large numbers of items in categories could be helpful in choosing the w_c. In this regard, we note that it is possible to specify a priori the v_c in equation 7 and then to determine the w_c from them (Dunnette and Hoggatt, 1957; Wilks, 1938).

Finally, we wish to emphasize that the w_c are chosen a priori to define a composite universe score. They are not necessarily chosen as the weights to be applied to observable category scores for estimating the composite. Typically, such estimation weights are chosen on the basis of some estimation criterion. For example, if a minimum error variance criterion is chosen, weights in the BLP function (or some other form of regression) can be used. In contrast, if an unbiased estimate for a particular examinee is desired, the w_c can be used to apply to the observable category scores.

Covariance Structure Models. Outside the generalizability framework, several covariance structure models have been suggested for studying categories implied by a table of specifications. Bock and Bargmann (1966) first discussed the application of a covariance structure model for the table of specifications problem, and Wiley and others (1973) generalized the Bock and Bargmann model in discussing similar issues. Subsequently, Mellenbergh and others (1979) suggested the use of covariance structure models in conjunction with Guttman's (1969, 1980) facet theory for analyzing tests. However, there is an important distinction between a multivariate generalizability perspective on tables of specifications and the structural models proposed by these authors. That distinction lies in the stronger assumptions that must be made for covariance structure models. Such assumptions are not implied by the much weaker assumption of sampling items from categories that is associated with a generalizability perspective.

Just as we do not require a structural model to hold exactly for a given sample of persons, the generalizability perspective does not require a structural model to hold exactly for a given sample of items. What the covariance structure models suggested thus far do not do is to consider a random dimension for items or some other facets; such a consideration allows us to claim that a structural model does not have to hold exactly even when observations from the entire population of persons are analyzed. Such a consideration is a fundamental aspect of generalizability theory, and it is a feature that makes multivariate generalizability models appealing for analyses of data associated with a table of specifications. Generalizability models refer to overall parameter values for a universe of items such that, for fixed categories (universes) of items, structural models can be specified for the categories; however, stronger assumptions are needed to specify structural models for given samples of items from these categories.

There seems to be some confusion about this in the literature. For example, Werts and others (1974) claim that covariance structure models can be used to test measurement assumptions that they mistakenly associate with generalizability theory. However, the measurement assumptions that they use are inconsistent with the fundamental basis of generalizability theory, namely the idea of sampling conditions of measurement. Even in the first exposition of the theory by Cronbach and others (1963), it is clear that the assumptions that Werts and others (1974) associate with generalizability theory are inappropriate. Again, covariance structure models have stronger assumptions than one would consider in a generalizability model. Perhaps the confusion is created by the well-known fact that covariance structure analysis can be used to estimate variance components (Bock and Bargmann, 1966; Linn and Werts, 1979). However, using such an analysis to compute estimates is quite different from requiring scores on sampled items or groups of sampled items to conform exactly to a structural model. Thus, the assumptions used in the multivariate generalizability models described in this chapter are not to be confused with the assumptions associated with the covariance structure models that have been proposed thus far for studying the same issue.

Random Sampling Assumptions. The notion of sampling items or conditions of measurement raises a question about the appropriateness of the random sampling assumption for items in each category of a table of specifications. Rajaratnam and others (1965) provide detailed arguments for viewing test construction as a stratified (categorized) random sampling process. By contrast, other authors have claimed that test construction practice defies objective description. However, in many measurement procedures, a major categorization of items can be described. Given such a categorization and the weak assumptions of the theory, multivariate generalizability seems ideal for modeling test construction effects. Indeed, random sampling of items within categories is a sufficient, but not a necessary, condition for most of the statistical assumptions in the models described here.

If random sampling within categories is not used in test construction, research on categories of items could be described as a process of rejecting hypotheses that claim that item responses are undifferentiated. Admittedly, when one starts with very weak assumptions, it can be quite difficult to reject hypotheses on the basis of empirical evidence. However, it should always be possible to reject any model on the basis of such evidence. In the present context, if there is any idea of a further categorization of responses that goes beyond some major categorization, then any research plan should consider the possibility of rejecting the simpler major categorization in favor of the more complex one. If random sampling within categories is in fact used for test construction, research into a further or different categorization of responses to items remains valuable, because it can lead to a more efficient stratified sampling plan.

Under circumstances in which random sampling is used, there remains, in generalizability theory, the assumption of independent response error. The models described here actually require the weaker assumption of uncorrelated response errors. If this assumption is violated, statistics based on categories of items can become quite meaningless. Let us consider a situation in which content categories of items are grouped together in a test; thus, examinees respond to items in one content area, then to items in another, and so forth. Clearly, observed covariances among item responses within a physical grouping can be higher than they are among responses across groupings because of content separation or because of correlated response errors within groupings. A simple experimental design can be constructed to determine whether response errors are correlated. However, it is much easier to obtain evidence that the assumption is violated than it is to model such correlations.

Content Characteristics and Statistical Properties of Test Forms. In constructing multiple forms of a test, one often hears it suggested that the multiple forms should have similar distributions of difficulty levels and discrimination indices. To the extent that this goal is achieved, the multiple forms are likely to be approximately parallel in the classical sense, and traditional procedures for equating scores on multiple forms will frequently result in relatively minor adjustments of observed scores. However, for test forms associated with a well-defined table of specifications, attempts to achieve idealized distributions of difficulty levels and discrimination indices are sometimes in conflict with the purpose of a table of specifications. For example, it is possible for two forms to have similar distributions of difficulty levels across all items in the two forms but for some content categories in one form to consist mostly of difficult items and the corresponding categories in the other form to consist mostly of easy items. Such a result seems clearly undesirable when one wants multiple forms to possess a high degree of content equivalence. This problem can be avoided in principal by exercising some degree of control over the statistical characteristics of items within categories. In short, it seems highly desirable for developers of multiple test forms to adhere to the content characteristics and other a priori aspects of measurement identified by a table of specifications and to exercise control over certain statistical properties of test forms.

In the example considered in this chapter, we took one table of specifications as given a priori and then developed and examined a model that incorporated effects associated with categories in that table of specifications. We also considered what would happen if test forms deviated in certain ways from the table of specifications. From a broad perspective, we might want to consider whether a particular stratification scheme was good, efficient, or optimal in some sense. This issue has received little treatment in the literature. For example, it is seldom recognized that items in different content categories of a table of specifications frequently exhibit different statistical properties. Also, with the exception of Linn (1980), few authors seem to have considered identifying operationally defined categories that result in differences in statistical properties of categories. Although this practice is inappropriate in some circumstances, it is difficult not to agree with the view that good test construction practice involves the development of an efficient stratification of items in the overall universe of generalization. In constrast, test construction that categorizes items on the basis of content or other a priori aspects of measurement but that subsequently ignores these categories to ensure statistical comparability across forms seems at best to have an inefficient stratification scheme. From this perspective, a major motivation behind our research on tables of specifications is ultimately to suggest improvements in test construction by identifying stratification schemes that improve statistical control while preserving the intended universe of generalization.

The model that we have considered and the example that we have discussed can be considered to be in the general area of internal consistency analysis. For example, we have concentrated on average statistics over multiple forms of a test, not on statistics about examinee responses to pairs of forms. Also, we have not incorporated occasion as a facet in our model or example. Thus, our results can be criticized for relying on such assumptions as uncorrelated response error, which was discussed previously. Our principal reason for restricting ourselves to what can be called *internal consistency analysis* is pragmatic. Given practical constraints, such as available testing time, and the impetus of current testing legislation, tending as it does toward release of test forms, it is difficult and expensive for such a testing program as the AAP to conduct a good study involving administration of two forms of a test to the same randomly sampled examinees, with or without an intervening time interval. In the event that such data are available, however, it is easy to expand the models that we have discussed so as to include additional relevant facets.

Some test administration modes do not rely as heavily on the assumptions associated with internal consistency analysis. For example, consider the situation in which separately timed pretest or preequating sections are administered along with an operational form of a test. These sections are often developed to parallel a subsection of the full test; so, they should allow a detailed analysis at the level of the table of specifications. (Jarjoura, 1981, used a pretest administration for estimation with the Natural Sciences subtest of the AAP.) Such an administration mode can also provide checks on assumptions of a model used for internal consistency analysis because of the separate timing of the sections. However, an occasion facet is still lacking.

Finally, the table of specifications that we have discussed has a rather common structure, but it certainly does not exhaust the possibilities, and certainly we are not suggesting that all test development procedures should be forced to fit this model. Indeed, we believe that the fitting should be in the other direction; that is, psychometricians should develop models that reflect particular test development processes with reasonable fidelity. The task of doing so can be complicated, but the use of simplistic models with complicated test construction procedures can result in relatively uninformative and misleading analyses. We suggest that applications of multivariate generalizability models such as the one considered in this chapter hold considerable promise at least for mitigating the discontinuity between many test development procedures and psychometric procedures that treat all items in a test as an undifferentiated set.

References

American College Testing Program. *Content of the Tests in the ACT Assessment.* Iowa City: American College Testing Program, 1980.

Bock, R. D., and Bargmann, R. E. "Analysis of Covariance Structures." *Psychometrika,* 1966, *31,* 507–543.

Brennan, R. L. *Elements of Generalizability Theory.* Iowa City: American College Testing Program, 1983.

Brennan, R. L., and Kane, M. T. "An Index of Dependability for Mastery Tests." *Journal of Educational Measurement,* 1977, *14,* 277–289.

Cronbach, L. J., Gleser, G. C., Nanda, H., and Rajaratnam, N. *The Dependability of Behavioral Measurements: Theory of Generalizability for Scores and Profiles.* New York: Wiley, 1972.

Cronbach, L. J., Rajaratnam, N., and Gleser, G. C. "Theory of Generalizability: A Liberalization of Reliability Theory." *British Journal of Mathematical and Statistical Psychology,* 1963, *16,* 137–163.

Dunnette, M. D., and Hoggatt, A. C. "Deriving a Composite Score from Several Measures of the Same Attribute." *Educational and Psychological Measurement,* 1957, *17,* 423–434.

Guttman, J. "Integration of Test Design and Analysis." In *Proceedings of the 1969 Invitational Conference on Testing Problems.* Princeton, N.J.: Educational Testing Service, 1969.

Guttman, L. "Integration of Test Design and Analysis: Status in 1979." In W. B. Schrader (Ed.), *Measuring Achievement: Progress Over a Decade.* New Directions for Testing and Measurement, no. 5. San Francisco: Jossey-Bass, 1980.

Jarjoura, D. *Variance Component Models for Content and Passage Effects in the English Usage and Natural Sciences Subtests of the ACT Assessment Program.* ACT Technical Bulletin No. 39. Iowa City: American College Testing Program, 1981.

Jarjoura, D. "Best Linear Prediction of Composite Universe Scores." *Psychometrica,* in press.

Jarjoura, D., and Brennan, R. L. *Three Variance Component Models for Some Measurement Procedures in Which Unequal Numbers of Items Fall into Discrete Categories.* ACT Technical Bulletin No. 37. Iowa City: American College Testing Program, 1981.

Jarjoura, D., and Brennan, R. L. "A Variance Components Model for Measurement Procedures Associated with a Table of Specifications." *Applied Psychological Measurement,* 1982, *6,* 161–171.

Joe, G. W., and Woodward, J. A. "Some Developments in Multivariate Generalizability." *Psychometrika,* 1976, *41,* 205–219.

Kelley, T. L. *Statistical Methods.* New York: Macmillan, 1923.

Linn, R. L. "Test Design and Analysis for Measurement of Educational Achievement." In W. B. Schrader (Ed.), *Measuring Achievement: Progress Over a Decade.* New Directions for Testing and Measurement, no. 5. San Francisco: Jossey-Bass, 1980.

Linn, R. L., and Werts, C. E. "Covariance Structures and Their Analysis." In R. E. Traub (Ed.), *Methodological Developments.* New Directions for Testing and Measurement, no. 4. San Francisco: Jossey-Bass, 1979.

Mellenbergh, G. J., Kelderman, H., Stiljen, S. G., and Zondag, E. "Linear Models for the Analysis and Construction of Instruments in a Facet Design." *Psychological Bulletin,* 1979, *86,* 766–776.

Rajaratnam, N., Cronbach, L. J., and Gleser, G. C. "Generalizability of Stratified Parallel Tests." *Psychometrika,* 1965, *30,* 39–56.

Wang, M. C., and Stanley, J. L. "Differential Weighting: A Review of Methods and Empirical Studies." *Review of Educational Research,* 1970, *40,* 663–705.

Werts, C. E., Linn, R. L., and Jöreskog, K. G. "Intraclass Reliability Estimates: Testing Structural Assumptions." *Educational and Psychological Measurement,* 1974, *34,* 25–33.

Wiley, D. E., Schmidt, W. H., and Bramble, W. J. "Studies of a Class of Covariance Structure Models." *Journal of the American Statistical Association,* 1973, *68,* 317–323.

Wilks, S. S. "Weighting Systems for Linear Functions of Correlated Variables When There Is No Dependent Variable." *Psychometrika,* 1938, *3,* 23–40.

Woodbury, M. A., and Novick, M. R. "Maximizing the Validity of a Test Battery as a Function of Relative Test Lengths for a Fixed Total Testing Time." *Journal of Mathematical Psychology*, 1968, *5*, 242–259.

David Jarjoura is a psychometrician at the American College Testing Program.

Robert L. Brennan is Director of Measurement Research at The American College Testing Program.

Index

NEW DIRECTIONS PAPERBACK SOURCEBOOKS

• Practical problem-solving aids for busy professionals
• Ideal educational and training resources for seminars, workshops, and internships

SINGLE COPIES
$7.95 each

when payment accompanies order. *Payment must accompany single copy orders under $25.00.* (California, New Jersey, New York, and Washington, D.C., residents please include appropriate sales tax.) For billed orders, cost per copy is $7.95 plus postage and handling.

BULK PURCHASE DISCOUNTS

For bulk purchases (ten or more copies of a single sourcebook) the following rates apply:
   10–49 copies $7.15 each
   50–100 copies $6.35 each
   over 100 copies *inquire*
Sales tax and postage and handling charges apply as for single copy orders—see above. Return privileges not extended for sourcebooks purchased at bulk order discount rates.

SUBSCRIPTIONS

$35.00 per year for institutions, agencies, and libraries.
$21.00 per year for individuals *when payment is by personal check.* (No institutional checks are accepted for the $21.00 subscription.) Subscriptions begin with the first of the four quarterly sourcebooks for the current subscription year. Please specify if you prefer your subscription to start with the *coming* year.

ORDER CARD

Please read ordering information in the left margin before filling out this order form. Other sourcebooks in this series are listed at the front of this book, along with additional details for ordering. *Prices subject to change without notice.*

Name (or PO#) _____
                (please print clearly)

Address _____

City _____

State _____ Zip _____

☐ Payment enclosed.   ☐ Bill me.

SINGLE COPY ORDERS. Enter sourcebooks by code (such as HE#2 or CD#5) and title (first two words).
Example: HE#2, Strategies for . . .

_____
_____
_____
_____

☐ **FREE CATALOGUE** describing sourcebooks in all sixteen *New Directions* series:

New Directions for Child Development
New Directions for College Learning Assistance*
New Directions for Community Colleges
New Directions for Continuing Education
New Directions for Education, Work, and Careers*
New Directions for Exceptional Children*
New Directions for Experiential Learning*
New Directions for Higher Education
New Directions for Institutional Advancement*
New Directions for Institutional Research
New Directions for Mental Health Services
New Directions for Methodology of Social and Behavioral Science*
New Directions for Program Evaluation
New Directions for Student Services
New Directions for Teaching and Learning
New Directions for Testing and Measurement

*Publication suspended for these series. However, individual sourcebooks are still available.

SUBSCRIPTIONS. Enter series titles and year subscription is to begin. Example: New Directions for Higher Education, 1983.

_____
_____

☐ Institutional, agency, and library. Each series: $35.00 per year.   ☐ Personal. Each series: $21.00 per year *(payable only by personal check).*

JOSSEY-BASS INC., PUBLISHERS
433 California Street • San Francisco 94104

BUSINESS REPLY MAIL

FIRST CLASS   PERMIT NO. 16103   SAN FRANCISCO, CA

POSTAGE WILL BE PAID BY ADDRESSEE

Jossey-Bass Inc., Publishers
433 California Street
San Francisco, CA 94104